NEW BRAZILIAN ART

Pietro Maria Bardi

NEW BRAZILIAN ART

PRAEGER PUBLISHERS
New York • Washington • London

Acknowledgments

The author and the publisher express their gratitude to Luiz Sadaki Hossaka for the general revision of the text; to the painters Willys de Castro and Hercules Barsotti for the revision of the index; to the architect Hermann Waldemar, archives of *O Cruzeiro*, Editora Abril and *Manchete*.

Photographs in this volume by:
F. Albuquerque, G. Baccaro, G. de Barros, R. Brandao, H.G. Flieg, M. Gautherot, E. Gonçalves, **A. Guthmann**, H. Henrotte, L.S. Hossaka, H. Merkel, S. Moy, J. Moscardi, O. Savio, T. Scheier, S. Scliar, F. Stockinger, M. Textor, U.D. Zanella.

BOOKS THAT MATTER

Published in the United States of America in 1970 by Praeger Publishers, Inc.
111 Fourth Avenue, New York, N.Y. 10003

© 1970 by P.M. Bardi

Library of Congress Catalog Card Number:
73-106816

Printed in the Netherlands

1 Visitors at an art exhibition at São Paulo, 1967 . Photo by José Xavier

Preface

It does not seem to have occurred to anyone before to make a general survey of the best that Brazil is producing in the field of the arts. The reason for this may perhaps be sought in the difficulty of making a selection at a time like the present when all values are caught up in a vertiginous whirl of change, and are consequently at the mercy of cliques who, because they have merely assumed the very latest fashions, believe themselves to be the legitimate representatives of the moment.

Moreover, the country is so vast and many-sided, so proliferous, that any attempt to select what might be of interest to foreign readers from the whole of a very large output becomes a difficult matter. In this survey I have therefore sought to bring together the leading personalities of the generation that has prepared the ground for a vigorous contemporary art, and those of the younger generation, who are now cultivating a plastic tradition rich in ideas and achievements. In order to show how the arts subsist in our country I shall also have to say something about the different atmospheres in which the various tendencies have acquired consistence.

In a survey like the present Brazilian art can only be classified in its wider aspects, and on strictly matter-of-fact lines. There are three main divisions. The first includes the art of the Indian tribes, practically limited to pottery and featherwork, and now, unfortunately, since the penetration of white civilization, produced largely for tourists. The second is the popular art of the countryside, which is produced in isolation, unselfconsciously, in the handicraft tradition, still pre-industrial-revolution, and consumed in the same environment it is produced in. The third division includes what may be called civilized and

122312

5

2 M.H. CHARTUNI. *Mother*, 1967. Oil on board and acrylic, 60×60 cm. Museum of Art, São Paulo

representative art, produced by professional artists according to their numerous categories and tendencies ranging from truly creative individuals to what one might call 'visual communicators', such as graphic and industrial designers, whose influence on the mass of the population is always the greatest.

In introducing an exhibition of young Brazilian artists belonging to the Paris School held at the *XX Siècle*, Jean Cassou, commenting on the saying that the School is a kind of America because it effects a transformation in the most diverse types of immigrants, observed that 'Brazilians are Brazilians above all for the great diversity of their origins. Each of them, in the midst of the mad confusion of the present world, is a destiny unto himself. America is the land of such destinies, and this very American America that is Brazil... And so, here or over there, these artists carry in themselves an adventure, a habit of taking risks, an inclination to uproot themselves no less than to take root elsewhere, a kind of pathetic liberty.' The truth about young Brazilian art – without preconceptions, free of encumbering tradition yet at times strongly attached to remote American or even colonial beginnings, or else to more recent social events, '...ranging widely between the extreme primitive and the extreme avant-garde' – could hardly have been more concisely expressed.

Such, then, is the field of action – a field of unlimited possibilities, which are taken for granted owing to a typically Brazilian feeling of liberty and spaciousness, with no prohibited areas, where tropical architecture could become so famous in so short a time, where painters could be launched who have won prizes at the Biennials of Venice, Paris, and Tokyo, and film directors who have triumphed at the Festival of Cannes.

As a result of this active presence of Brazilian art in the international field it would seem that a certain demand has arisen in various quarters for information of a more comprehensive nature, and it is this want that the present volume is intended to fulfil.

3 J.A. DA SILVA. *Sugar-cane plantation (Life and work and wealth – Viva Brazil!)*, 1950. Indian-ink drawing, 82 × 150 cm. Collection: Mirante das Artes, São Paulo

Introduction

Brazil is bewildering. Even the visitor who has plenty of time and is able to work out unusual itineraries away from the beaten tracks of the tourists soon finds that he is confronted with a whole combination of elements – natural, economic, human, spiritual – upon which he will be unable to form a consistent opinion unless he has collected a great deal of accurate, detailed, and unhurried information from the country's past and present history.

In nearly all books by travelers (apart from those that merely deal in such platitudes as 'country of the future', 'land of contrasts', 'sprawling cities', 'mineral resources', and the like) judgement is defective and hardly more than commonplace, even when it has not already been distorted or confused by recourse to tendentious sources, political or religious. In this immense plateau interwoven with rivers and forests, or even in the cities themselves, it is not at all difficult to lose one's way in trying to arrive at general conclusions; it will be more profitable, therefore, to leave philosophic speculation aside and turn our attention to the realities of Brazilian life by making direct contact with people of all social classes, where simple data may be gathered that really have some tangible value.

Yet such encounters invariably yield contradictory information, which must be callrefuy considered in the light of the enthusiasm and disillusion of a permanently expanding country and of the habit of solving problems by trial and error – problems which, as in many other nations nowadays, involve popular passions too easily set ablaze, less easily extinguished, and difficult to restrain or control.

The first reliable conclusions that can be drawn will concern the national character, which includes a peaceful disposition, a tolerant humanity, none of the baseness that comes from racial strife, a feeling of nationhood, an almost fatalistic confidence in being able to survive adversity, a liking for poetry, a

4 G. SAMICO. *Leaf-Eater*, 1964. Woodcut, 50 × 70 cm. Museum of Contemporary Art, São Paulo

natural bent, native and autonomous, for art. Brazil is made up of many little realms whose vague frontiers do not prevent the existence of a certain cultural unity – a spiritual, or rather supernatural, existentialism, which refashions religions to its own taste, mixes them up, transforms and corrects them when necessary, invents new liturgies, fashions, forms, and colors.

It being the purpose of this book to describe all those activities implicit in life, some useful, some super-fluous, that go under the name of art, the first thought that comes to mind is to go to the people who live far from the cities, to their household objects, their images, their tools, and finally to their ingenious misuse – which may even be unconsciously ironic – of the products of machine civilization for such simple purposes as decoration, lighting, or toys.

This has nothing to do with folk-lore, which is quite a different matter; it is, rather, a question of in-genuity, of the art of creating something charming as well as useful with spontaneity, and with none of the intellectual attitude that now, in the frantic search after novelty for novelty's sake, has taken to regarding commonplace, everyday objects as things to be elevated, by fantastic manipulation, to aesthetic dignity and invested with strange new values that go by the name of Pop art.

Side by side with this natural art of the people there is, of course, another – in fact, *the* other – art, the so-called civilized art, refined by its practitioners and offered to top people, the art you read about every day in the newspapers, with all the usual names, and the usual hoax of the picture that turns out to have been painted by a donkey with a brush tied to its tail.

Thus we have two sullen, impassive sphinxes, each of them too proud to acknowledge the existence of her companion. She of civilized art represents the intellect at work at its fullest capacity; she of popular art stands for ordinary good sense, which gets itself less talked about. If one were to make a purely quantative comparison, the former would be a microscopic sphinx, but in her representative capacity she is immense.

Then there is a third sphinx who has got into the picture: industrial art, thrust in like a hyphen between the two of them. In the opinion of those sociologists who see nothing but catastrophy in store for humanity her magnitude, by virtue of what is called the progress of civilization, is destined to become total, for she will swallow up the other two, and the whole population without exception will be served by mass-production, and the only artists allowed to exist will be industrial designers.

5 Indians painting each other in preparation for a ceremony . Photo by M. Javurek.

Indian art

It should not be forgotten that n some areas of Brazil there are Indian tribes still living in the Neolithic age and producing works of handicraft in pottery, wood, stone and feathers according to primeval traditions in spite of the influence of white civilization – which is always detrimental, unfortunately. A Government Indian Protection Service ensures some degree of independence to this type of production, which is, nevertheless, becoming enfeebled by natural exhaustion. In regions where contacts with the outer world are more limited and controlled by specialist ethnographers the craftsmanship maintains much of its pure, primeval character. Indian art has had little influence on the development of Brazilian art, for apart from the remoteness of these oases of primitive art, and the difficulty of reaching them, they have not been visited by explorers of the requisite talent and interpretative ability. When the Indians worked for the Jesuits in the building and decora-tion of churches there was some cross-fertilization between native and European styles, but it produced little of interest. Heirs of Andean civilizations migrated down the Amazon towards the Atlantic, and some of these tribes, such as the Tapuyans, the Cuna, and those of the Marajoan culture, failed to escape the slaughter of the colonists and are now extinct; others, like the Carajás, the Tapirapés and the Bororos, have survived, and they produce among themselves an art that lends this profile a touch of the archaic; yet it is up to date as well, since the distinction between 'barbaric' and civilized art is no longer made. Thus there exist side by side in Brazil today both very ancient traditional forms of art and, as we shall see in the following pages, forms of a popular art which has developed in jungle isolation and has resisted, and to some extent still resists, the transformations imposed by mechanical progress.

6

7

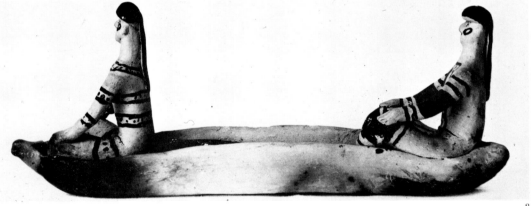

8

10

9

6 Indian tribesmen shoot poisoned arrows against the airplane that has spotted them in the impenetrable Amazon jungle. Photo by J. Manzon.

7 Model boat allusive of the Aruaná dance of the Carajá tribe.

8 and 9 Carajá art, Goiás state. Statuettes of painted sun-baked terracotta. Photos by G. Grovelli

10 Tucuna art, upper Solimões river. Necklace pendant in coco-nut shell.

11 Tucuna Indian, upper Solimões river, painting a tondo on bark for the Feast of the New Girl an initiatory rite).

12 Another Tucuna necklace.

13 Feather headdress of a Carajá Indian, Aragnaia river, used at the feast of the initiation of adolescent girls, when two small circles are tattooed on the cheeks.

14 Basket in rushwork of the Tirujó tribe, Xavantina region.

15 Anthropomorphic ceramic of the Marajoan region.

16 Waurá Indian, Batovi village, on the Xingú river, with roucou-dyed hair, toucan-feather ear-pendants, and jaguar-claw necklace.

17 Tucuna art. Painting on bark.

Photos 10-12, 14, 15 by G. Rossi, 13, 16, 17 by H. Schultz.

10

12

14

15

11

13

16

17

18 Small-town life in the north-east, in the open space where an occasional circus is the only form of theatrical entertainment. Photo by P. Verger.

Popular art in Brazil is mostly concerned with the simple and traditional facts of the countryside. A spontaneous naturalness is evident in the works of elementary construction and architecture, in handicrafts and art, and in the carved and painted ex-votos, which are animaned by a highly characteristic philosophy which achieves the union of the Roman Catholic faith with native superstition—until technology breaks in. When it does, in the form of cans, the man of the Sertões turns his hand to making:

19 Oil lamps, from tin cans. Paraiba state. Collection: L. Bo, São Paulo.

18

19

Popular art

Brazilian popular art must be considered region by region: there is the coastal region (sub-divided into north and south), the interior plateau region, and the Amazonian region. Each covers an immense area, has its own peculiar characteristics, its own racial make-up, its own types of tools and household implements; and even such universal manifestations as religious ceremonies, or the carnival, have certain features not common to all. The fishing vessel called a *jangada*, a beautiful example of boat-building, is peculiar to the north. On the São Francisco river the Indian canoe has been replaced by an entirely different kind of craft fitted with a *carranca*, a talismanic and luck-bringing figurehead. In the south boats have Mediterranean forms.

Pottery provides another example of regional differences. In the state of Pernambuco it has a dramatic figurative liveliness and may be regarded as an art; in the other regions it is purely utilitarian except for some geometrical decoration. The varieties of basket-work, of musical instruments, of building materials, of clothing (which, in the interior, is entirely of leather and designed to meet the requirements of the *vaqueiro*),

are numerous, and reveal the restless temperament of the craftsmen who produce them.

To enter a wayside chapel and see what popular art is capable of inventing, from the altar itself to the sculptures, the paintings, the embroideries, the lamps, the infinite variety of form and color of the ex-votos, is to come into contact with a world so alien from our own that it seems quite impenetrable.

Brazil has a splendid and varied heritage of this kind of art, the spontaneous result of a long history, originally purely indigenous but subsequently influenced ethnographically first by the African influx and then by the mass-immigration of Europeans. Each people added its legends and memories to the common stock of humors, temperaments, sorceries, images, and imaginings, which has become part of the vivacity of the nation. It has blossomed out into a spectacle of form and color, of contrivancies and novelties, which have very much the same characteristics as those that are more familiar in the music that has emerged from the same milieu. Take the samba, for instance, a dance brought by the Negroes from Luanda which, combined with the in-

fluence of other profane and religious dances, has become a riot of rhythms and lyrics with a highly poetic flavor, in which numerous witty themes are being continually given new forms and new words, so building up a rich treasury of songs.

In considering Brazilian art as a whole, therefore, it should be borne in mind that the popular element, whose importance was discovered and which was defended by the Modernists in the twenties, may well provide the same sort of new blood that the exoticism of Asian and African art had brought to the highest forms of civilized art in Europe. For had not Paris successfully revitalized with such new blood, and with primitive content, the worn-out art of officialese country themes and urban anecdotes that had fallen into a dead end of senile soliloquizing? In Brazil, where the cities are too cosmopolitan for an aesthetic renewal of this description, recourse has been had to the exoticism in the country itself. I shall have something to say later about the chief participants in this enterprise.

Some idea of the extraordinary abundance of the fruits that flow from the cornucopia of popular art, whose plastic productions are entirely un-

20

21

22

23

24

25

20 Example of a common type of Brazilian dwelling of the colonial period, the so-called House of the Bandeirante at São Paulo, of the pioneer, that is, who gave Brazil her geographical and economic identity. Probably built in the seventeenth century, and recently restored, the house is a prototype in that it represents the best solutions of the problems of space, use of available materials, and functionality. A baker's oven is in the foreground.
21 Grater for producing manioc meal, the basic food of the country people. The walls of the house are of daub reinforced with saplings.
22 Sugar press, with a plough in the background, and a large earthernware vessel to the right.
23 Another sugar press.
24 Earthernware market at Agua de Meninos, Salvador, Bahia.
25 Chapels of vernacular construction at Palmeira dos Indios, Pernambuco.   Photos by G. Rossi.

known abroad, or even in the south of Brazil, may be gained from one or other of the translations of a recent novel by Guimarães Rosa, *Grande Sertão: Veredas*, in which the author describes, through the confessional monologue of a former *jagunço* (a legendary type of libertarian and anarchic rebel from civilization), a whole universe of things, and of passionate and religious states of mind, which are modest in themselves but intensely dramatic, and evidence of a deep yearning for immortality; he writes to such effect that one is lost in admiration of his style and astonished at his exposure of such unrevealed aspects of the human psyche. It is, however, a world that has also been penetrated to some extent by young film-makers such as Glauber Rocha, with *Deus e o Diabo na terra do sol*, and Nelson Pereira dos Santos with a film taken from *Vidas Sêcas*, a novel by Graciliano Ramos, which is written episodically, somewhat in biblical fashion, and tells of a nomad family which lives on sun,

impassivity, fatigue, thirst, hunger, and death.
The existence of a primitive way of life is one of the realities of Brazil, and the question of protecting the authenticity of popular arts and customs, or of whether they can be adapted to the new, machine civilization, has recently been the subject of some controversy. Preservation activities have been centered on the Museum of Popular Art at Salvador, Bahia, which its founder, Lina Bo, intended to be not just a record and depository of objects but a permanent example meant to clarify ideas about the old dilemma of Brazilian art: whether to look for it at home or abroad. According to Lina Bo, 'in the next ten or perhaps five years Brazil will have drawn up her cultural plans and chosen a particular programme to be followed: she will have to become either a culturally autonomous country, built on its own foundations, or an ungenuine country with a pseudo-culture copied from imported and unsuitable systems, a sham version of other countries'

cultures; a country in a position to take an active part in the universal concert of cultures, or a country hankering after other surroundings, regions, and climes. Brazil today is divided between two tendencies: one to keep abreast of the world, ever looking abroad, trying to pick up all the latest novelties in order to relaunch them upon the cultural market hastily smartened up with a national varnish; the other to look inward on and around herself in the difficult search among the scant heritage of a new and passionately loved land for the roots of a culture which is still without form, and to foster it with a seriousness that admits of no levity.'
It will be appreciated, therefore, that in this vast and in many ways unknown country the problems of cultural, and consequently artistic, definition are more than a few. Popular art is a reality that cannot be ignored in this connection – hence the necessity for this brief description.

26

27

28

29

26 Salvador. Street-procession, in Indian costumes, of the carnival club 'Sons of Gandhi'. Photo by G. Verger.
27 Popular ceramic art, Pernambuco region, representing primitive sugar manufacture.
28 Exhibition of the Popular Art of Bahia State, São Paulo, 1959, organized by L. Bo and M. Gonçalves.
29 Commemorative portrait of the zebu 'Turbante', first prize at an agricultural show, Morrinhos, Goiás, 1966. Oil on zinc, 30 × 40 cm.
30 Caruarú, Pernambuco. Ceramics stall in the market.
31 Toy, Pernambuco region.
The collection and study of handicraft objects, both old and new, has received much attention in recent years, especially in the north where, for historical reasons, the most characteristic types are to be found. Through the enterprise of Lina Bo, the Museum of Popular Art was founded at Salvador in a group of seventeenth- and eighteenth-century buildings which were adapted and restored for the purpose.

30

31

32

33

34

32 One of the rooms in the Museum. In the foreground, wooden mortars.

33 General view of the Museum buildings, which are still known by their original name, da União. In the background, the 'solar', or master's house; in the foreground, the church, deconsecrated in the last century and later turned into a small hotel.

34 Another room in the Museum, section for objects made from tin cans, wood, and earthernware.

35

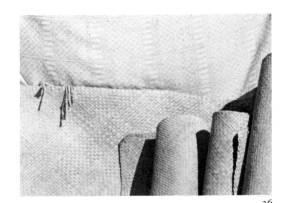

36

37

38

39

40

FOGUETES

41

AGUARDENTE
LEÃO DO NORTE

ANÁLISE Nº.

MARCA REGIST.

PROCEDÊNCIA ESTADO DA BAHIA
ENGARRAFADORA: INDÚSTRIA BRASILEIRA
ORGANIZAÇÃO LEÃO DO NORTE LTDA.
SALVADOR - Pç. ADRIANO GORDILHO S.N. (BÔA VIAGEM) - BAHIA

42

ELIXIR DOS REUMÁTICOS

CANINHA TATUZINHO

o melhor aperitivo nacional

43

PARATY
TANGARÁ
DELICIOSA AGUARDENTE

MARCA REGIST.

INDUSTRIA BRASILEIRA

PRODUZIDO PELA
ORGANISAÇÃO LEÃO DO NORTE LTDA.
SALVADOR - BAHIA

44

INDUSTRIA BRASILEIRA   TEOR ALCOOLICO ATÉ 54º

LEITÃOZINHO

REG. Nº I.F Nº 7455

PRODUTO DO ESTADO DE SÃO PAULO

45

46

INDÚSTRIA BRASILEIRA   PRODUTO DO EST. DE S.PAULO
CANINHA
"TATUZINHO"
RÓTULO E MARCA REGISTRADA
L.C.C.D.M.A. Nº 973 CONTEÚDO
PURA E   DELICIOSA
REGISTRO no
Aguardente de Cana
Adoçada   Grad. Alcool. até 54 GL.
ENGARRAFADA POR
D'ABRONZO SOCIEDADE ANONIMA
Av. D. Maria Elisa, 44   PIRACICABA   Fone - 4480
Registrado no S.P.A.P. sob nº 19.875 - Registrado no I.F. sob n° 5.488

47

ESPECIAL AGUARDENTE DE CANA
ADOÇADA
REGIST. Nº S.P.A.P.   TEOR ALCO. ATÉ
SOB Nº 30367   54º GAY LUSSAC
PURÍSSIMA
PIRACICABA   VILA REZENDE
AVENIDA RUE
BARBOSA Nº 340   TEL. 3244
ENGARRAFADA POR
C.A.R. MIGNANI S.A.
IND. E COMÉRCIO DE BEBIDAS   CONT. MIN. 660 ml

48

VILA
ASSUMPÇÃO   CAFÉ NHA PENTA

49

50

Popular commercial art in Brazil is of great variety but of elementary iconography. The general convention is to make use of the figure of the Indian for advertising fireworks, of various animals for ardent spirits, of flowers for medicines. The leaf and the berry of the coffee-plant are also very popular. What is remarkable about this form of art, produced by the co-operative efforts of improvised artists and primitive printing plants, is the curious combination of ingenuousness and shrewdness.

41–50 Labels of popular branded goods from various parts of Brazil.

35 Group of ex-votos in wood, some painted. Collection of the Ceará State University, Fortaleza, displayed in the Gallery of Modern Art in Rome, 1966, for an exhibition of popular Brazilian art, which did not, however, take place.

36 Rush mats, Pernambuco region.

37 Carranca, or figurehead, São Francisco river. Museum of Popular Art, Salvador. When the canoe was replaced by Mediterranean types of craft in the first half of the last century, the prows were fitted with carved figureheads representing animals propitious for good sailing.

38 Group of ex-votos in wood, plain or painted, from the northeast, at an exhibition in the Museum of Modern Art, Rio, 1966. Private collection, São Paulo.

39 Anchors made by fishermen of the northeast from stones, wood and lianas.

40 Fishing-boats known as jangadas, an original type invented by the northeasterners.

Woodcuts illustrating booklets of popular songs and ballads which are sold at fairs and markets and make up a rich corpus of 'string literature', as it is called, the booklets being slung over lines of string stretched between trees. The words are declaimed to groups of listeners, and deal with legends, historical and current events, and even politics.

51 Python swallowing a Government official.
52 The *Cangaçeiro* (gentleman bandit) and his bride on horseback.
53 The cat with seven heads.
54 The *Cangaçeiro* before St Peter at the gate of heaven.
55 Young man changed into a serpent.
56 Girl changed into a bitch.
57 Girl scared by the Devil.
58 Serpent-girl.

51

52

53

54

55

56

57

58

The work of the popular artists is a mixture of spontaneous ability and adjustment to practical solutions. As there is 'string literature', so there is improvised music based on elementary harmonies, and ingenuous painting which tells stories and turns out landscapes. But since Brazilian primitivism in the arts, in the wake of the fashion that passed through Paris before the war, is regarded as a trend, it has produced large numbers of neo- and pseudo-primitives, who are of no interest and who, as with any other passing fashion, merely get in the way. Speaking of the Brazilian primitives, José Augusto França has justly pointed out that even artlessness can be learnt, just like anything else, and he cites the *Carta apologética e analítica pela ingenuidade da pintura*, 1725, by the Portuguese Joseph Gomez da Cinz, in which it is argued that painting cannot be produced by naïfs. True, but have we the courage to admit it?

18

59

60

61

62

63

59 DJANIRA. *Drying Coffee Beans*, 1938. Oil on canvas, 69 × 97 cm. Collection: Gilberto Chateaubriand, Rio.
60 M. G. PALMA. *Fatal Encounter with Sucurí the Serpent-Monster*, 1940. Oil on canvas, 46 × 71 cm. Collection: F. Stockinger, Pôrto Alegre.
61 J. A. DA SILVA. *The Cotton Harvest*, 1948. Oil on canvas, 50 × 100 cm. Museum of Art, São Paulo.
62 I. DE ASSIS LADEIRA. *Currency Note*, 1965. Oil on canvas, 44 × 100 cm. Private collection, São Paulo.
63 H. DOS PRAZERES. *Return from the Plantation*, 1948. Oil on canvas, 35 × 53 cm. Collection: Buck, São Paulo.

64

65

66

67

69

70

68

71

72

73

20

64 E. B. DA SILVA. *Madonna with Angels.* Terracotta, height 18 cm. Museum of Art, Olinda, Recife.

65 R. DE OLIVEIRA. *Last Supper,* 1965. Oil on canvas, 80 × 100 cm. Collection: Norma Geyerhahn

66 A. MAIA. *Ex-votos,* 1965. Oil on canvas and collage of altar cloth, 46 × 60 cm. Private collection, Rio.

67 W. DE DEUS SOUZA. *Funeral of Raimundo de Oliveira,* 1966. Oil on canvas, 44 × 53 cm. Collection: Mario Schenberg, São Paulo.

68 C. M'BOY. *Flight into Egypt,* 1950. Oil on canvas, 117 × 81 cm. Museum of Art, São Paulo.

69 T. D'AMICO. *Dona Janaina* (Afro-Brazilian folk goddess), 1959. Collage of lace, sea-produce, cotton and painting, 41 × 41 cm. Private collection, São Paulo.

70 G. DE SOUZA. *Offerings,* 1965. Oil on canvas, 30 × 50 cm. Collection: Arturo Profili, São Paulo.

71 F. D. SILVA. *Animals Fighting in the Amazon Jungle,* 1965. Collection: Mirante das Artes, São Paulo.

72 G. ALVES DIAS. *Beach at Olinda,* 1966. Oil on canvas, 41 × 65 cm. Collection: Baby Moraes Pinto, São Paulo.

73 A. B. DE FREITAS. *The Ipiranga Palace at São Paulo,* 1963. Oil on canvas, 50 × 60 cm. Collection: Mirante das Artes, São Paulo.

74 T. DO AMARAL. *São Paulo,* 1925. Oil on canvas, 66 × 89 cm. State Picture Gallery, São Paulo.

The approach to modernity

We have so far seen something of two of the components of Brazilian art: the art of the Indians, which bears witness to the presence of people who still represent and keep alive, to some extent, the indigenous culture of the land, and the art of the common people, developed during four centuries of immigration from both Europe and Africa, with the resulting mixture of races, which also amounts to what is practically a native culture in itself. It is now time to see how a third component evolved and took shape: the so-called civilized art, isolated from ethnographical influences and unconcerned with the extemporizing and force of circumstance that limit popular art. The presence of this third component cannot be ignored in a general survey like the present, but it deserves to receive particular attention at the moment because it is the other two that receive all the sympathy of the younger generation of Brazilians, anxious to discover sentiments of nationality in their own history, almost as a defense against the international style as it becomes always more generalized and aggressive. Primitive painters are highly esteemed in Brazil today, they represent the nation in exhibitions abroad, and symbolize the interest that the Brazilian has for art—particularly painting and music.

Brazil, in colonial times, gradually assuming the features of civilization after the Iberian model, accepted but modified the styles of the art it imported. The Baroque came from Portugal, but it was adapted to the tropical scene till it amounted, at times, to a reform of the standard rules, as the case of Aleijadinho shows. It was only after the move of the Portuguese Court to Rio, and after the arrival of a mission of French artists invited by the King in 1816, that art entered the scene as a profession and as a factor in social life, with all due consequences. With the establishment of a Fine Arts Academy Brazil suffered the same fate as all the other South American countries: she became a tardy participant in the afterglow of a late Romanticism. Only after the First World War did Brazil begin to catch up with Europe, and to take part in the avant-garde movements centered on Paris.

1922-1945

75 R. BRANDÃO CELA. *The Abolition of Slavery*, 1938? Oil on canvas, 300 × 520 cm. Ceará State Government Palace, Fortaleza.

Any discussion of Brazilian art, which now presents itself to the world as belonging to the so-called modern generation, must begin with a note about the preceding generation, the generation that fought the campaign to bring Brazil as up to date in the arts as other countries. Some of those who took part in the movements that appeared after World War I, as a result of cultural exchanges which had finally broken the bounds of fusty academicism, are still taking an active part in the affairs of today, alongside the younger men to whom they have frequently been teachers and protectors. In fact, in a new nation made up of immigrants from very diverse peoples and more accustomed in the past, where the arts were concerned, to submit to the dictates of academicism rather than risk the abrupt breaks with tradition that were being continually proposed beyond the ocean, the process of bringing Brazil up to date was to encounter various difficulties; and conventionalism, some aspects of which are still a force in Latin America today, was not the least of them.

At the time of the Captaincies, and even after the arrival of the royal family of Portugal, who came as refugees and made the country an empire, Brazil was divided into regions, which were almost completely isolated from each other. Although federation was helped to some extent by the unity of the language, a certain separatist tendency continued even after the proclamation of the Republic, and artistic activity went on in watertight compartments, without, however, acquiring the regional characteristics that were becoming manifest in other fields. The same phenomenon may be observed in other countries, as for example in Italy, where the Risorgimento produced only a provincial art.

It is, of course, only too true that there can be no general agreement as to which of the various movements is to be taken as representing the 'national' art. In Italy, before World War I, a nationalist movement, *Strapaese*, was in conflict with a cosmopolitan one, *Stracittà*, Futurism wanted to destroy the museums and art galleries, and later Mussolini discovered the 'modern Roman style'. The *status quo* of nineteenth-century Brazil was one of sleepy tranquillity, the tranquillity of art schools functioning in every region after the pattern of the Academy, founded by the French artistic mission of 1816 under the insignia of romantic neo-classicism.

It was not until about 1920 that Brazil woke up to the fact that she was behind the times. The first to make the discovery were the 'Modernists'. Certain unknown poets thought it was time to express themselves in terms other than those of the Parnassians or the Symbolists; young writers became enchanted with the great variety of our landscape, our tales and legends, as a change from the conventionalism of the Romantic movement; sociologists appeared and began to investigate the origins of Brazilian society, going back to the first colonial adventurers and studying the social system and way of life that grew up among the patriarchal, slave-owning families; a group of artists began to visit Europe in search of all that was most sensational and controversial.

The shade of Benedetto Croce forbids us to indulge in historical ifs, but it is safe to say that the academic mission of 1816 did a good deal of harm. Brazil had had certain nonconformists before then, inspired by pro-native and autonomist—even anti-colonial—sentiments, especially in the Minas region where goldmining and the discovery of diamonds had brought sufficient prosperity to support the arts. Small but splendid towns, like Vila Rica (now Ouro Prêto), São João del Rei, Diamantina, and Mariana, were provided with magnificent churches, the extraordinarily inventive sculptor and architect, Aleijadinho, was active, and a small 'Mineiro' group of poets appeared as an expression of Brazilian nationalism. Three of the group, in fact, were involved in the libertarian movement of 1789: Cláudio Manoel da Costa, who committed suicide, and Tomás Antônio Gonzaga and Alvarenga Peixoto, who were deported to Africa. (The leader of the movement, Tiradentes, was hanged.) They were not the first poets to suffer exile: a century earlier Gregorio de Matos had been exiled for writing the following epigram:

> The Brazilians are fools
> Working away like slaves
> All their lives to keep
> The Portuguese knaves.

These are not events to be overlooked, for art and poetry, in the regions that were already established in the eighteenth century, were not only characterized by patriotism, lack of race prejudice, and humanitarianism, but also by a desire for independence and a determination to manage on one's own. When the Modernist movement started in the twenties its members looked abroad,

76 E. VISCONTI. *Providence Guides Pedro Alvares Cabral to the Discovery of Brazil*, 1899. Oil on canvas, 182 × 109 cm. State Picture Gallery, São Paulo.

but they did so only to gain information, to discover up-to-date techniques, to make contacts and seek ideas that might be useful to apply at home, and not to accept things passively like ready-made imports. The moving spirit of these activities was naturalistic. Nor had Brazilian writers, even in the nineteenth century, wholly cut themselves off from the outer world; they, too, had looked abroad. The ones who absolutely failed to see or understand anything at all were the painters. The poets, however, saved the nation's honor. In 1836 they even published a magazine in Paris called *Nitheroy*, in the first number of which it was asked why on earth the Olympian deities should be made to invade the skies, the forests, and the rivers of Brazil. In attacking this Arcadian and outlandish classicism imported via Lisbon, Gonçalves de Magalhães asked 'Can Brazil inspire the imagination of poets?' The answer was that she could, and Romanticism stepped in, clothing itself with the indigenous mythology. The legends of Homer were bid farewell and local legends welcomed in their place. After the study of Indian lore came the discovery of the landscape, the Empire was cleaned up by the abolition of slavery, and the old Portuguese paternalism shaken off. A beneficent Positivism arrived and inscribed 'order and progress' on the national flag. The pages of Gonçalves Dias and Castro Alves, as well as those of José de Alencar, showed that Brazil was growing up rapidly, in a climate of republican liberty and mass immigration, and starting on the difficult transition from a rural to an urban and industrial society.

It was a hard struggle. A new social structure was taking shape and becoming recognizable. From time to time the transatlantic liners disembarked a few artists among the immigrants, each of whom took part in and contributed whatever he had, which was not always very much, to the development of taste in the capital. But no rebellion, not even an isolated voice, was raised against academicism. The ruling class was content with vast patriotic subjects, demure portraits, and small genre paintings. Order, but no progress. On the other hand, poetry, the well-loved art that none can do without, which the common people have cultivated from time immemorial listening to the ballad-singers in the marketplaces, sought new modes of expression, freed itself from metrical purism, and brought its vocabulary up to date. In a word, it foreshadowed renewal.

The Modernist movement was a poet's movement, therefore, before it was joined by painters, sculptors, musicians or architects. The inevitable route to this new world led through Paris, a city much loved by the families of the landed aristocracy, who spent their holidays there, taking along their servants and household linen, and returning with French furniture, bronzes, paintings, perfumes, bibelots, wives, marvellous dresses by Poiret, and a French *r* in their pronunciation. The ultimate snobbery was to have one's shirts sent to Paris

77 Unknown artist. *The Proclamation of the Republic of Brazil*, about 1889. Oil on canvas, 82 × 102 cm. Private collection, São Paulo. This painting suggests the popular artist's predilection for historical scenes, which were to become the most characteristic mode of expression of the academic painters, who undertook vast paintings—almost dioramas—glorifying political and martial occasions in the life of the young nation; among them the name of Pedro Américo de Figueiredo is remembered.

for laundering. The drama, music, and fiction that found favor were all French. The *hors concours* painting of the Salons entered by the front doors of their Rio and São Paulo houses decorated in the ribbony style of the period.

All this was before 1914. When the cataclysm was over, Brazilian visitors to the Ville Lumière found there had been great changes: Chabas replaced by Picasso, Rodin by Brancusi, Mallarmé by Apollinaire, at the height of his fame; and the music of Ravel and Debussy was almost popular. The Brazilians, like all Americans for that matter, realized, after the periods of Cubism, Futurism, and Dadaism, that the world had taken to new ways of thinking, and that an unending series of isms were on their way. Would it be possible to import, adapt, and make use of them exclusively as modes of expression? It was a critical situation, and needed careful handling if a complicated system of communicating vessels containing different cultures, involving risks of mutual contamination, dangerous contiguity, or alienation of autonomous values, was to be kept under control. It was like an infantry engagement, when the final result only becomes clear after the fighting is over. As it was, the situation was not saved without some burnt fingers. Nevertheless, the presence of two considerable artists helped to

avoid serious accident, and once again the national spirit, enthusiastic in its self-confidence, a certain self-acquired taste, ingenuity, and genuineness, prevailed. The two artists were Mário de Andrade and Heitor Villa-Lobos. They proclaimed themselves adherents of primitivism, and sought to preserve without change an archaic and familar tradition. Later, their group would be unable to hold out against foreign penetration and the adoption of an international style, as has happened everywhere.

Mário de Andrade's poem *Macunaíma*, which is unfortunately untranslatable into other languages owing to the very distinctive nature of the local tropical soil that nurtured it, exemplifies all the necessary conditions for a national, autonomous poetry: not to consider things outside the country, to study our own affairs among ourselves, to give expression to our own feelings, our own domestic dreams, and to write for ourselves and as we understand ourselves. But he was a poet who was also a stimulating critic with a mind open to all the arts, and he exerted a fascinating influence on the growing activities of the contingent that kept making visits to Paris.

All this activity went on between São Paulo and Rio de Janeiro. The north did not appear on the scene until later, although some individuals

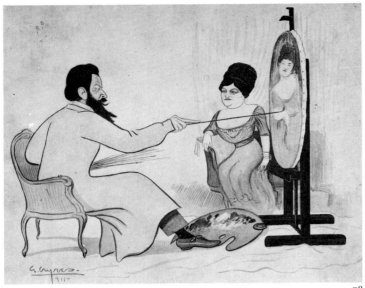

78 79

80

78 and 79 E. CARDOSO AYRES. *The Ladies' Portraitist* and *The Lady Reciter*, 1911. Pencil-and-wash drawings, 19 × 24 and 21 × 16 cm. Private collection, Recife. Cardoso Ayres was the sharpest observer of the Brazilian middle classes, whom he urbanely but implacably satirized after the manner of the Parisian Sem.
80 Classroom in a school of fine arts, Salvador, at the beginning of the century: drawing lesson with geometrical solids. Art instruction on the Brazilian states followed closely, but tardily, the methods of Paris.

who had come south from Recife were among the participants of the original breakthrough—the Week of Modern Art held at São Paulo in 1922. This was a spectacular event with art shows, concerts, lectures, poetry readings, and prose recitals, given to rowdy audiences somewhat after the fashion of Marinetti's 'Futurist evenings', and not without some throwing of deteriorated food-stuffs. Making due allowance for differences of time and latitude, the Week was rather like that first exhibition of the Impressionists at Nadar's.

It seems that the original idea was due to the painter Emiliano Di Cavalcanti, although the real promoter and liberal financier was Paulo Prado, coffee-grower, sociologist, and highly esteemed intellectual.

The intention of the movement was to launch anti-academicism, to revise values. 'A risky business', said Mário de Andrade, 'owing to its extreme boldness, its violent nationalism, its unpopular gratuitousness, its arrogant dogmatism.' In a city where nothing had ever happened,

except for two avant-garde exhibitions that came and went amid little more than cordial silence, it created a scandal. The organizers and those invited to take part did not all share the same ideas. Among them were René Thiollier, the secretary, a conservative gentleman of polite and formal manners, afterwards secretary of the São Paulo Academy of Letters; Menotti del Picchia, an agreeable writer and, for the occasion, a metaphysical painter; Ribeiro Couto, an *intimiste* poet after the manner of Francis Jammes; Ronald de Carvalho, first a Parnassian and then a follower of Walt Whitman; Oswald de Andrade, who favored a 'modernist Indianism', which he later proclaimed as a theoretical system; Cassiano Ricardo, a pastoral poet somewhat in the style of the Italian 'crepuscular' school; and others of various tendencies, including Guilherme de Almeida who, when it was all over, declared that it had been nothing but sheer buffonery, dealt out just as it came, without any critical awareness, 'no program, no manifestoes, no leaders, no nothing', the only purpose being to welcome, as the Romantics had done, the new *mal de siècle*, namely international modernity, multifarious also at home 'by virtue of its own vital necessities'.

Young exegetes today are of a different opinion, however: '...salutary Brazilian intuition, close to the earth, in contact with the people. Of imported matter there was almost nothing, whereas one of the triumphs of this poetry was the conquest of Brazil herself'—is the view of J. G. Merquior. In fact, Modernist poetry succeeded in imposing itself on Brazilian sentiments, as was shown by the most original of the poets of the time, Raul Bopp, author of a wild lyric poem *Cobra Norato*. The Week's guest of honor was the poet Graça Aranha, who opened the proceedings with a speech attacking the Brazilian Academy of Letters, of which he was himself a member. It was one of the most useful contributions to the controversy. He slated the arbitrary rules of abominable 'good taste' and sterile 'good sense', and called for independence and liberty of expression against parochialism and 'melancholy of the race'; he was evidently influenced to some extent by the art-for-art's-sake doctrine. Two years later, the same poet conducted a spirited campaign to free the Brazilian language from subservience to Portuguese and to prevent the country's being made into a 'mortuary chamber of Portugal'.

As we have seen, there were various kinds of interests in play, and various kinds of objections to them. Nevertheless, the Week was the klaxon call that sounded the advance towards the conquest of a new culture. ('Klaxon'? The word was the title of a magazine published for a while soon afterwards.)

As might have been expected, the secessions began almost immediately. The most curious concerned Mário and Oswald de Andrade, and was due to the intransigence of Mário, a strict Roman Catholic, when confronted with Oswald's

Style and art in the first quarter of the century.
81 A. PARREIRAS. *Allegory of Sculpture*, 1925. Palace of Liberty, Belo Horizonte.
82 Fashions on the fazenda.
83 'Garibaldi' cigarette carton.
84 and 85 Advertisements.
86 Graphic art styles in common use up to about 1930.

87

88

The style of architecture in Brazil, before the arrival of European architects, or of Brazilian architects who had studied in Europe, was much the same as it was everywhere else; the pseudo-style of Eclecticism was dominant.
87 Detail of a decorated house at São Paulo, first decade of the century. Photo by A. Vigliolia
88 Art Nouveau revolving door at São Paulo, early twentieth century. Photo by José Xavier.

proclaiming the necessity of divorce—which furnishes another example of the fortuitous nature of the group. Immediately after the Week Oswald published his manifesto on Anthropophagism, of the purest naturalistic orthodoxy: 'Language with no archaisms. No erudition. The millenary contribution of error... Instead of naturalistic humor, synthesis. Instead of fluency, invention and surprise.' The sermon went on defiantly in a firework display of witticisms: 'Against all the importers of canned consciences... World without dates. Unindexed. No Napoleon. No Caesar.' But the writer, like all the other conspirators, except Mário de Andrade, was raving mad to get to Paris and come back full of ideas, of paintings by Léger, de Chirico, and Picasso, and with guests like Blaise Cendrars. The links between São Paulo and the 'Café of Europe' became extremely close. The go-between was Tarsila do Amaral, a young painter who, after having put in some hard brushwork at the Académie Julian (the Parisian goal of every single one of the Brazilian painters who had preceded her), became a convert to Cubism, adapting it to Anthropophagism, though in a feminine manner and with the delicacy of a girl's posy at her first communion. She is the most talented of the Brazilian artists, and has discovered that Brazil needs painting in pure, heraldic colors—clear blues of the sky, tender greens of the banana foliage, the fiery red of the toucans. We can already perceive a national quality in her art, whose technique and execution derive from her master Léger.

Another lady painter, Anita Malfatti, went, instead, to Berlin, where she studied under Lovis Corinth. She had already exhibited some strange figure paintings in 1917, whereupon the most open-minded writer of São Paulo, Monteiro Lobato, had branded their touching and innocent schoolgirlish expressionism as 'mystification or paranoia'. Opinion was against anything that could not be interpreted as easily as a picture post card, and anyone who tried to swim against the stream deserves to be remembered. A real *enfant terrible* was Flávio de Carvalho, an iconoclast painter and a Cubist architect. On his return from England, where he had studied architecture-he suggested that light, easy-fitting tunics might be a more suitable attire on the Tropic of Capricorn than starched shirts, double-breasted suits, and hard hats. He was howled down. On one occasion he was nearly lynched by the crowd when he wanted to see what would happen if he did not remove his hat at the passing of a religious procession; on another he opened a theater where so much freedom was allowed that it had to be closed by the police.

One of the most active of this new generation of artists was Di Cavalcanti, mentioned earlier. He studied a little on his own, and a little in Paris. His subjects evoke the life of the people, carnival scenes, mulatto girls, streets full of samba dancers —the plastic correlative of that spontaneous music which is rooted in the semi-educated life of the cities, is renewed year by year, lends sound to tales and events, and furnishes the occasion for glittering spectacles. Di Cavalcanti is certainly the

outstanding figure of the generation that undertook to create the conditions in which free expression might flourish. He holds the balance between adherence to our own subject-matter and the acceptance of modes of expression divorced from the usual *beaux-arts* dullness, and he successfully steers a difficult course between social art and the allure of snobbery.

At this point it will be necessary to go back some years to an event that now seems almost ancient history. In 1913 the Russian painter Lasar Segall arrived from Germany and showed some of his work in a shop in São Paulo. He fell in love with Brazil, and after experiencing Expressionism in Berlin and Dresden, and being favorably noted by Will Grohmann, he returned to this country, where his ideas, and the argument they provoked, were far-reaching in their effects, and where he became noted for his high standard of professional ethics.

In about 1930, therefore, the leading artists in São Paulo were the incomparable Mário de Andrade, the eccentric Flávio de Carvalho, the beautiful Tarsila do Amaral, Anita Malfatti, Lasar Segall, Emiliano Di Cavalcanti, and the architect Gregori Warchavchik, whom we shall meet later on. There was a salon in the house of a kind lady who had decided to encourage the new art—Olívia Guedes Penteado. Here discussions were held and the profits and losses of the traffic with Paris were estimated. Then, as São Paulo was growing at a visible rate due to prodigious economic expansion, the Modernists moved to a club, which was less exclusive and more suitable for making proselytes.

89 Custom House at the port of Paranaguá, 1913.
90 The Municipal Theater, São Paulo, 1910. Architect Ramos de Azevedo. (From *Impressões do Brazil no século vinte*, London, 1913.)
91 Villa at São Paulo (from *O Estado de São Paulo*, Barcelona, 1918).
92 Pharmacy at Pelotas, Rio Grande do Sul, (from op. cit., London, 1913).
93 Project for the Banco Pelotense, Pôrto Alegre (from op. cit., London, 1913).
94 Drawing of São Paulo's first large department store.

89

90

91

92

93

This was in 1932, and the club was called the Sociedade Paulista de Arte Moderna. Exhibitions were held, with works by Vuillard, Picasso, Léger, Gleizes, Gris, the pictures being raffled among the members; festivities, especially carnival balls, were organized, with grandiose decorations by Segall; concerts of modern music were given, as well as readings and lectures. The enterprise deserves to be remembered, for it was one of the most effective attempts to take up a position against refractory opinion, led, where the arts were concerned, by a group of reactionaries highly organized for the counter-attack—which came with the Society's being dissolved by the police.

Like ants that are always ready to rebuild their demolished nest, the Modernists came together again, and in greater numbers, to continue their activities with a May Salon, organized on the lines of the Salon des Indépendants, at first under the direction of Quirino da Silva and later under that of Flávio de Carvalho. The manifestoes were embellished with maxims by Mondrian, and to make it doubly clear that it was intended to maintain contact with abroad the catalogues included passages in English, such as '...new horizons of plastic expression, assimilating and reproducing the meaning of the history of art of our time, in its technical progress and its sentimental, ideological and poetic contents.'

All this fervid activity on the part of the artists was reflected in the periodical press thanks to intelligent writers like Sérgio Milliet, Geraldo Ferraz, and Luís Martins, who obtained accep-

94

95

97

96

98

99

95 R. BRANDÃO CELA. *Father Anchieta Teaching Brazilians the Catechism*, 1930? Fresco. Ceará State Government Palace, Fortaleza.

96 Packet design for Tupy cigarettes, *c.* 1920.

97 M. SANTIAGO. *The Amazons*, 1923. Oil on canvas, 114 × 146 cm. Collection of the artist.

The cult of the Indian had many followers who interpreted in their own ways the warning of one of Brazil's greatest writers, Euclydes da Cunha (1866–1909): '...we must forget what is false and uncharacteristic in our mental make-up, which is particularly inclined to react in ways foreign to the genius of our race. We think too much in French, or German, or even Portuguese. Nearly a century after political independence we continue to live in total spiritual subjection. From the building of a sentence to the ordering of our ideas we show an excessive respect for the precepts of the exotic cultures we find so marvellous, which induce in us, a priori, singular states of consciousness, and which blind us to the essential aspects of our life so that our real character escapes us, being clothed in other attributes which take away from or smother its original nature.'

98 Design on a box of ointment. The Indians' shields symbolize the protection afforded by medicine against the attacks of disease. Pharmacia Freitas & Cia., Rio, first decade of the century.

99 T. BRAGA. Design for a tessellated floor inspired by the ceramic art of the Marajoan Indians in the natural dyes used by them—*genipapo*, *carajurú* and *tabatingas*, to be executed in Pará woods.

tance for the innovators. São Paulo was slowly coming up to date, and the traditional temple of the die-hard conventionalists, the Salon of Academic Art, had perforce to suffer the existence of one of Modern Art. In course of time the attitudes became modified, and now the two Salons open their doors once a year to distribute an enormous quantity of medals, and have been left behind by events that have made São Paulo famous throughout the world.

So far I have purposely confined myself to São Paulo, but we must now see what had been going on, meanwhile, in the capital. Rio de Janeiro, an old city with *élites* in every field, jealous of its traditions, which were the result of the nation's history and found expression in the academies, was very suspicious of 'avantgardism'. It had poets and writers of real worth, but exercised a damping effect on any new departure in the plastic arts. Eliseu Visconti, a painter of real genius, was completely muffled by the stuffy stay-at-home atmosphere in which he had to work. São Paulo was against the Modernists through provincialism; Rio through conscious conservatism. However, the Paulistas, as we have seen, invited the poet Graça Aranha from the capital to lend more importance to their Week. Such a manifestation would have been quite out of place in Rio. Mário de Andrade, who was not indifferent to sentiments of national unity, thought that the protest ought perhaps to have been made in the capital, but he came to the conclusion that

100 J. C. BRITO. *The Mother of the Waters*. Cover for a book by Herman Lima, 1920.

101 H. A. SEELINGER. *Carnival Allegory*, from the review *Fon-Fon*, 1909.

102 *Chastity*. Statue in a Salvador street, first decade of the century.

103 The cover of *Mademoiselle Cinema*, which led to the book's being banned after protests by the League of Morality, Rio, 1924.

100

101

it would have been impossible: '...there is no traditional aristocracy, merely a very wealthy *haute bourgeoisie*, which would never accept a movement that might endanger their conservative and conformist mentality. The *bourgeoisie* was never a good loser, and it is this that will be its downfall.'

But there was no lack of artists and poets in Rio eager to prepare the way for better times. The surrealist Ismael Nery became known only after his death. Celso Antonio, a promising pupil of Bourdelle and a vigorous sculptor, did not achieve success. Some years had still to run before the Minister of Education, Gustavo Capanema, was to invite Le Corbusier to show Rio the way to the new architecture—years during which the most outstanding personality of Brazilian painting, Cândido Portinari, was beginning to make a name for himself.

Portinari, born of Italian immigrants, came from a small town in the state of São Paulo and pitched his tents in Rio. He was a many-sided artist, and one of his ambitions was to become a mural painter so that he might infuse new life into Brazilian history painting as Diego Rivera had into Mexican. He became the visual reporter of the life of the Brazilian poor: crowds of boys playing football, boys on bicycles delivering laundry, scarecrows, kites flown by children against stormy skies, the life of the laborers on the fazendas, weddings and funerals of poor and humble folk. And he became Brazil's national painter: he could paint the First Mass said in

102   103

104

Brazil as readily as the Martyrdom of Tiradentes, and in a new, affable, cordial manner like that of a man of the people who speaks with few adjectives; and with his kindly revolutionist's heart he always addressed himself to the common people. More than any other artist, he was responsible for giving inspiration to Brazilian art, not always, perhaps, as an anti-traditionalist, but always ready, on his return from his trips to Europe, to take account of the innovations that Cubism or Expressionism had brought to the visual arts. Portinari also wrote some poetry characterized by intense human feeling—which is, indeed, the character of the Brazilian people themselves.

In the north things went differently, due both to differences of character and to remoteness from the two cities I have been speaking of. At the time of all these controversies means of communication were a factor to be reckoned with: nowadays one flies from Rio to Recife in a few hours; then it was a sea voyage of some days and quite an adventure. Recife, too, is a city remarkable for its history and art, and here a young man who concealed a perennial passion beneath an appearance of Goethian calm conceived the idea of regarding colonial history disinterestedly and investigating its ethnographical and social development. I refer to Gilberto Freyre, the author of one of the masterpieces of Brazilian literature, *Casa-Grande & Senzala* and its sequel *Sobrados e Mucambos* ('The Masters and the Slaves' and

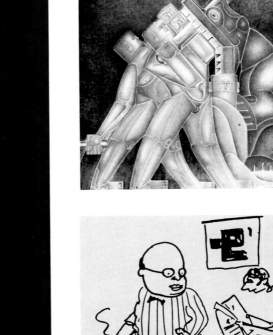

106

107

105

30

108

'The Mansions and the Shanties'). Professor Freyre represents the mentality of the north, and he has taken a leading part in art polemics since publishing a manifesto, in 1926, in defence of 'regionalism'. In it he assumed such a determined attitude that the usual devout conservatives—those of what the Brazilians call the let-it-be-and-wait-and-see mentality—advised the President of the Republic to regard it as an overt political act in favor of separatism, even though it contained the following declaration of principle: 'The exponents of this new kind of regionalism want to see other regionalisms establish themselves in the country in addition to that of the north-east, that the movement may assume a character that is organically Brazilian, even American, the most comprehensive…' The targets of this attack were, above all, foreign mannerisms in literature and the arts, and even in daily life, including the cuisine, which was derived from the Portuguese, imagined to be the best in Europe. Instead, in order to defend values and traditions 'from the danger of being altogether lost, such is the neophyte frenzy of those in charge whom we think of as up to date and progressive because they blindly copy foreign novelties', he was all in favor of a return to the roots that had nurtured the true spirit of Brazil through so many stormy vicissitudes. A very well-founded part of his attack was directed against urbanization of the Broadway type, against the rejection of an architecture that contained, even in the shanties, a highly significant combination of the rational and

108 T. DO AMARAL. *Anthropophagy*, 1929. Oil on canvas, 125 × 142 cm. Private collection. São Paulo.
109 T. DO AMARAL. *Abá-Porú*, 1929. Oil on canvas, 85 × 73 cm. Private collection, São Paulo.
110 T. DO AMARAL. *Oswald de Andrade*, 1922. Pastel on canvas, 47 × 36 cm. Collection: W. D. Lee, São Paulo.

109

110

111 A. MALFATTI. *The Russian Student*, 1917. Oil on canvas, 78 × 62 cm. Museum of Art, São Paulo.
112 F. DE CARVALHO. *Portrait of a Lady*, 1937. Oil on canvas, 74 × 60 cm. Collection: Mirante das Artes, São Paulo.
113 F. DE CARVALHO. *Psychological Self-Portrait*, 1936. Plaster of Paris, height 40 cm. Museum of Modern Art, Salvador.
114 Q. DA SILVA. *João Caetano*, 1929. Plaster of Paris, height 120 cm. João Caetano Theater, Rio.
115 Cover of the Catalogue of the Third May Salon, São Paulo, 1939, designed by Flávio de Carvalho.
116 Q. DA SILVA. *Landscape*, 1924. Oil on canvas, 37 × 37 cm. Collection of the artist.
117 N. MOURAO. *Shantytown Scene*, 1940. Pen-and-ink drawing, 40 × 47 cm. Collection of the artist.

111

112

the fanciful, and against the destruction of the greenery of the old colonial gardens and orchards. The essence of Gilberto Freyre's manifesto was his love of a patriarchal, fairy-tale Brazil that so-called civilization has largely destroyed with all the procedures of pseudo-progress such as land speculation, industrialization, mass-culture, and so on. Not that he wanted to halt progress; he wanted only to reconcile nature, history, and the traditions and spirit of the land with a conscious respect for order and for what ought to go under the name of progress. One of his artist friends, Cícero Dias, a delightful painter of Pernambucan life in scenes of pure and simple lyricism yet evocative of the most characteristic local color imaginable, has now in Paris, unfortunately, become an uninteresting abstractist. The matter of 'regionalism' goes far beyond the particular case of Recife and affects the whole question of Brazilian art, which is divided, today, according to the fashionable tendencies, between a small group of 'spontaneous' painters and a great horde of followers of the 'international style'—as will be seen from this survey.

It may be noted that Gilberto Freyre's manifesto,

113

114

115

116

117

which was close to the ideas of Mário and Oswald de Andrade, bore fruit about ten years later with the setting up of the Service for the National Historic and Artistic Patrimony whose purpose was to preserve what monuments of the past, especially architecture, had been spared by time and vandalism. The task of organizing the Service fell to Rodrigo Melo Franco de Andrade, and he saved some magnificent monuments of Colonial Baroque.

Among other northeasterners may be mentioned the poet Manuel Bandeira, who holds a leading position as the bard of Brazilian life, humor, irony, desperation, and melancholy; Lula Cardoso Ayres, a painter who has succeeded in extracting from the folk-lore and life of the people, and from the secrets of the mansions, a thematic idiom expressed with unique vivacity and understanding; the graphic artist Luís Jardim; and Vicente do Rego Monteiro, who was attracted to Paris, where he later distinguished himself in the Post-Cubist movement. He became the true representative of Brazil in the School of Paris, was on intimate terms with the masters, and always busy with numerous enterprises: he founded the magazine *Montparnasse*, brought Parisian painters to Recife, penetrated the forests to make a film on Dr Bougrat's escape from Devil's Island, became the owner of a distillery for the production of a special type of ardent spirits, went backwards and forwards to Europe, painting, poetizing, teaching—always in action. Somewhat further south, at Salvador, capital of the state of Bahia, a city with a long history and the seat of an ancient university, the modernizing movement was non-existent. Suffice it to say that in 1936 the exhibition of a Modernist painter, João Guimarães, was closed down following protests.

I have kept the question of architecture for the end of this note, since the movements I have been describing were almost wholly concerned with poetry and painting (although Villa-Lobos was mentioned in view of the fame he had acquired throughout the world). At the time of the Week, architecture, as an art, was in the hands of practitioners who merely reproduced the culturalistic styles of nineteenth-century Europe. Brazil had had no time to think about any aesthetic revival in the building trade. For certain reasons common to the whole of South America, architecture, which at the time of the formation of the Republics had escaped the influence of Neo-Classicism, except, perhaps, for some distant echoes of the Empire style dear to Napoleon, was abandoning itself to the most uninhibited and uncontrolled decoration of façades. The builders slavishly copied designs from books published in the European capitals. In the Baroque period, on the other hand, they had used prints for their models, but they had altered and adapted their lines in such a way and with such vivid and effective feeling that their buildings acquired the

118

119

120

Di Cavalcanti is one of the most popular painters because he has always been the commentator of everyday Brazilian life. He is intentionally anecdotal, and the episodes he catches with his sharp eye nearly always involve the provocative mulatto girls, whom he has characterized with a type that has become symbolical. But Di Cavalcanti has also given us fifty years of constant incitement and example in favor of an art that should be free of entrenched academicism. To the foreign reader his style may, perhaps, seem

conservative enough, but it should be seen in the context of the milieu in which he worked.

118 E. DI CAVALCANTI. *Birth of Venus*, 1940. Oil on canvas, 54 × 60 cm. Collection: Buck, São Paulo.
119 E. DI CAVALCANTI. *Girls of Guaratinguetá*, 1930. Oil on canvas, 100 × 74 cm. Museum of Art, São Paulo.
120 E. DI CAVALCANTI. *Mulatto Girl*, c. 1960. Oil on canvas, 72 × 54 cm. Private collection, São Paulo.

121

122

124

121 I. NERY. *Family of the Artist*, 1927. Oil on canvas, 75 × 68 cm. Private collection, São Paulo.
122 I. NERY. *Nude*, 1927. Oil on canvas, 77 × 57 cm. Private collection, São Paulo.
123 A. GOMIDE. *Brazilian Landscape*, 1925. Gouache on paper, 53 × 31 cm. Private collection, São Paulo.
124 I. NERY. *Portrait*, 1925. Oil on canvas, 69.5 × 78.5 cm. Private collection, São Paulo.

123

typical and individual character that has determined the special nature of Ibero-American architecture, so exciting and so varied from place to place. The few architects who afterwards came to Brazil adapted themselves to hybrid styles without realizing that a distinctive style might have been derived from the simplest form of colonial architecture, that of the rural dwelling. Not even the arrival of Art Nouveau drawings and illustrations had any effect: one might have expected, for instance, the substitution of the banana flower for the lily and the consequent development of 'Tropical Floral'. Except for a few examples at São Paulo by the architect Dubugras, Art Nouveau left no mark. Meanwhile, two new opera houses were being built, one at São Paulo, one at Rio, slightly simplified versions of the Paris Opéra, and such was their success that an enormous monument was erected to their architect, Ramos de Azevedo.

One or two voices were raised to plead that something ought to be done about architecture. Rino Levi, while still a student, wrote a letter to the newspaper, *Estado de São Paulo*, in defense of the 'modern', advocating 'convenience and economy, architecture of volumes with few, but sincere and well-emphasized, decorative

125 L. SEGALL. *Banana Plantation*, 1927. Oil on canvas,
85 × 124 cm. State Picture Gallery, São Paulo.
126 L. SEGALL. *Nude Female Bust, c.* 1920. Pencil
sketch, 57 × 43 cm. Segall Museum, São Paulo.
127 L. SEGALL. *Brazilian Landscape*, 1927. Water-
color, 48 × 66 cm. Segall Museum, São Paulo.

125

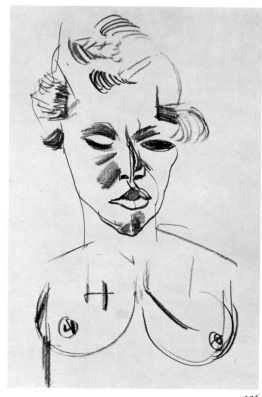

126

127

elements. No disguising of the structure of the building to obtain disproportionate effects... which amount to falsehood and artificiality... The old styles and the old systems have had their day.'

The moving spirit was the young Russian already mentioned, Gregori Warchavchik, who had taken his degrees in Rome and emigrated to Brazil, taking with him his rationalist ideas which had failed to find fertile soil even in Italy. He built his own house at São Paulo, purely linear, and in defiance of the regulation that houses should have pitched roofs. This was the first scandal. A bigger one followed with the construction of the 'Modernist House', which was shown to the public, furnished with Bauhaus-style furniture, and works of art to match, and which provoked the strongest objections from the conservatives. But the breach had been opened. Together with Lúcio Costa, Warchavchik started the movement that was later to become known as the 'Brazilian style', and in due course to be characterized by the plastic inventiveness of Oscar Niemeyer.

That this radical break with tradition became possible was due to a combination of circumstances. In the first place, Le Corbusier, in 1936, was invited to give a series of lectures in Rio de Janeiro, and these lectures gave rise to heated discussions. Secondly, it was just at this time that a competition had been advertised for a new Ministry of Education building, and everything had seemed to indicate that the capital was about to have one of the usual barrack-like edifices

128

129

130

131

132

covered with a lot of irrelevant decoration so dear to the hearts of bureaucrats and politicians. Instead, a miracle occurred. Getulio Vargas was then President, and his Minister of Education was Gustavo Capanema. By a dictatorial act the competition was set aside, Le Corbusier designed the building in its general lines, and a team of young architects—Lúcio Costa, Oscar Niemeyer, Affonso Reidy, Carlos Leão, Jorge Machado Moreira, and Ernani Vasconcelos—was charged with the execution. The Ministry, built in defiance of the antiquated and harassing town-planning laws, represents one of the major victories of contemporary architecture, and with its realization Brazil immediately joined the few pioneer countries in this field.

Notwithstanding his habitual modesty, the large part played by Lúcio Costa in the building of the Ministry, and in the architectural revolution in general, is well known. He himself observed, it may be remarked, that the event was also of significance from a sociological point of view, and a reason for optimism and hope, for the repercussions noted abroad showed that there could now be no denying that the Brazilian genius had finally proved its worth. Foreign influences had, in fact, been assimilated, without ideological servilism, and in certain aspects even surpassed in the execution.

The Ministry building, begun in 1937, was still under construction when other examples of the new architecture began to appear in various cities. Younger men who had studied with Costa and Warchavchik, and become fully converted to modern design, were now starting on their careers. This transitional period was one of violent

128 and 129 The drawing-room (no longer in existence) of Dona Olívia Guedes Penteado at São Paulo, where the group that had taken part in the Week of Modern Art used to meet. On the walls and about the room, paintings and sculpture by Lipchitz, Brecheret, Segall, Léger, and Brancusi; the decoration was by Segall.

130 E. DI CAVALCANTI. Caricature of Mario de Andrade (leader of the Week of Modern Art), 1928 (from História da caricatura no Brasil by H. Lima).

131 GUEVARA. Caricature of the Poet Manuel Bandeira, 1928 (from the review Para Todos).

132 Poster for a dance organized by the S.P.A.M., São Paulo, 1934.

133 L. SEGALL. Decoration for a ball at São Paulo, 1928.

134 Title-page of *Poemas analogos*, by Sérgio Milliet, 1927.

135 Invitation to carnival festivities from the S.P.A.M., São Paulo, 1933, designed by a follower of Segall. The Sociedade Paulista de Arte Moderna took a strongly anti-bourgeois line, at times provocatively so, as when it organized masked balls in which conservative attitudes were satirized, and even came to being denounced in the press as a 'dangerous den of debauchery'. The best of its members were the musicians, Camargo Guarnieri, Francisco Mignone, Souza Lima, the pianists Antonieta Rudge, Guiomar Novaes and Dinorah de Carvalho, and the famous dancer Chinita Ulman. Among the others were the music critic João Caldeira Filho, Mussia and Carlos Pinto Alves, the painters J. W. Rodrigues, Vittorio Gobbis, Hugo Adami and John Graz—apart from the names already mentioned in the text.

136 L. SEGALL. Decoration, 1928.

137 Cover of the Catalogue of the Second May Salon, São Paulo, 1938. Lino cut by L. Abramo.

controversy, for the vested interests of 'official' architecture, especially those closely linked with the old bureaucratic machinery, did not fail to do everything they could to prevent the success of the innovators. But Brazil then had a dictatorial regime which cannot be denied due credit for a large part of the achievements in this field.

At the same time as the building of the famous Ministry, a group of highly qualified and intelligent young men, the Roberto brothers, built the headquarters of the Press Association at Rio, using systems of climatic defense and conditioning that showed considerable advance on Le Corbusier's own *brise-soleil*. The Santos Dumont airport was built, also by the Roberto brothers, and the seaplane station according to a simple design by Attílio Corrêa Lima. At São Paulo the Esther block of flats by Alvaro Brazil marked the be-

ginning of a really modern architecture. Recife also had a new-style building: an atomic research laboratory by Saturnino de Brito. All these cases served to arouse an absolutely unprecedented interest not only in architectural problems in general but also in the question of functionality, which was now being agitated. Acceptability from the aesthetic standpoint was to be helped forward considerably by the original garden architecture of Roberto Burle Marx.

These, in brief outline, are the events that took place in Brazil between the two wars; I shall have something to say later on about what has happened between the end of the last war and the present, when we shall meet again some of the names of the so-called 'patriarchs'—those of them who are still active today.

As if the country's immense problems did not exist, a calm and peaceful Brazil was depicted by numerous artists between the two wars who were unworried by problems of content and unaffected by current trends and tendencies. It being impossible to name them all, a few may be selected as an example.

138 C. OSWALD. *Circle of Cypresses*, 1920. Aquatint.

139 L. FICKER. *Figures*, 1936. Woodcut, 20 × 13 cm.

140 H. FEIJÓ. *Land-Workers in Pernambuco*, 1945. Oil and ink on paper, 60 × 100 cm. Collection: M. Gonçalves, Rio.

141 P. LAU. *Sugar-Cane Workers*, 1937. Woodcut, 13 × 8.5 cm. Whereabouts unknown.

142 Q. CAMPOFIORITO. Tempera sketch for a mural, Rio, 1941.

143

144

143 C. PRADO. *Night Street Cleaners*, 1935. Oil on canvas, 100 × 120 cm. Museum of Art, São Paulo.
144 O. GOELDI. *Solitaire*, c. 1935. Woodcut, 25 × 30 cm. Collection: A. Profili, São Paulo.
145 A. GUIGNARD. *Ouro Prêto*, 1950. Oil on board, 60 × 100 cm. Museum of Art, São Paulo.

146 A. TERUZ. *Children's Football*, 1940. Oil on canvas, 50 × 61 cm. Collection: Epifánio Bittencourt, Rio.
147 C. DIAS. *River Bathers*, 1930. Water-color on paper, 57 × 41.5 cm. Collection: Mirante das Artes, São Paulo.
148 J. PANCETTI. *Seascape*, 1945. Oil on canvas, 33 × 24 cm. Collection: Buck, São Paulo.

145

146

147   148

149

150

At São Paulo, between the two wars, a group of landscape painters of various tendencies, some of whom are still active, came together under the name of the 'Family of Artists'. The most outstanding of them, the veteran Alfredo Volpi, today one of Brazil's most appreciated painters, has developed through a phase of Concretism towards synthetic forms that are almost heraldic.

149 A. VOLPI. *Houses by the Sea*, 1952. Oil on canvas, 70 × 45 cm. Collection: Theon Spanudis, São Paulo.

150 A. VOLPI. *Houses*, 1952. Oil on canvas, 45 × 60 cm Collection: P. and J. Nemirovsky, São Paulo.

151 M. ZANINI. *Church of São Vicente at Santos*, 1938. Oil on canvas, 50 × 70 cm. Private collection, São Paulo.

152 F. PENNACCHI. *Village Square*, 1940. Oil on board, 50 × 75 cm. Private collection, São Paulo.

153 C. GRACIANO. *School Scene*, 1962. Oil on canvas, 280 × 300 cm. Collection: Editora Brasil, Salvador.

154 A. BONADEI. *Milho*, 1952. Oil on canvas, 50 × 39 cm. Private collection, São Paulo.

155 F. REBOLO GONZALES. *Children of Morumbí*, 1935. Tempera on canvas, 80 × 65 cm. Whereabouts unknown.

156 P. ROSSI OSIR. *Seascape*, 1940. Oil on canvas, 53 × 64 cm. Museum of Art, Olinda, Recife.

151

152

153

154

155

156

The whole aim and purpose of Portinari's art was to give expression to his violent social commitment, to put on record certain tragic aspects of Brazilian life. He was thus exposed to the danger of falling into the idiom of the mere illustrator, and in fact his youthful ardor lost some of its fire in later years.

157 C. PORTINARI. *Black Madonna*, 1935. Oil on canvas, 60 × 73 cm. Collection: P. and J. Nemirovsky, São Paulo.

158 Part of the first Portinari retrospective exhibition organized by the Museum of Art, São Paulo, 1948. In the background, three paintings: '*Retirantes*', *Funeral with Net*, *Dead Child*.

159 C. PORTINARI. *St Francis*, 1944. Mural in the Church of Pampulha (architect, O. Niemeyer), Belo Horizonte.

160 C. PORTINARI. *Scarecrows*, 1940. Oil on canvas, 80 × 100 cm. Private collection, São Paulo.

157

158

159   160

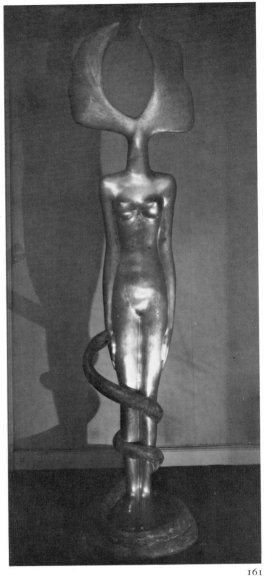

161

162

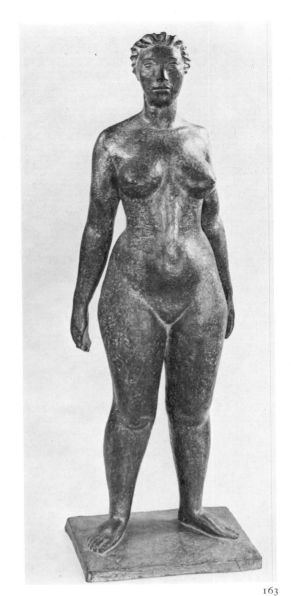

163

164

161 M. MARTINS. *However*, 1950. Bronze, height 300 cm. Collection of the artist.

162 M. MARTINS *Ritual of Rhythm*, 1960. Bronze, height 500 cm. Gardens of the Palace of the Dawn, Brasilia.

163 J. FIGUEIRA. *Nude*, 1929. Bronze, height 70 cm. Private collection, São Paulo.

164 B. GIORGI. *Dead Hero*, 1961. Bronze. Collection of the artist.

165

166

167

168

165 E. DE FIORI. *Warrior*, 1940. Plaster of Paris, height 91 cm. Museum of Art, São Paulo.

166 CELSO ANTONIO. *Nude*, 1927. Bronze, height 91 cm. Private collection, São Paulo.

167 A. ZAMOYSKI. *Portrait of the poet Jan Kastrowicz*, 1913. Wood, height 30 cm. Museum of Art, São Paulo.

168 A. ZAMOYSKI. *Self-Portrait*, 1915. Plaster of Paris, height 55 cm. Whereabouts unknown.

169 August Zamoyski's atelier at Saint-Clair-de-Rivière, H.-G., France, where he now lives. In the background, a statue in stone, *The Shadow of the World*, 1937–48. Among the benefits of the Polish sculptor's long residence in Brazil, particularly in the field of technical instruction, was the atelier which he set up in Rio and ran on co-operative lines and which turned out some of the best statues and monuments of the time.

169

170 G. WARCHAVCHIK. House at São Paulo, 1927. It is generally believed that the new architecture in Brazil is due exclusively to the impact of Le Corbusier at the time of his visits. But it should be remembered that the first promise of a new style came from the Russian architect, Gregori Warchavchik, whose early works, which met with so much opposition, are illustrated here as *incunabula*.

The new architecture

Having briefly surveyed the history of the generation that was responsible for the birth of the new epoch, we must now see how the various groups and their individual members involved in the movement of renewal became active and developed what is now recognized as a distinct and national style—with particular reference to architecture. It is in architecture, in fact, that Brazil, reciting the creed introduced by Le Corbusier, but in the language of a traditional experience rich in native idiom and modes of expression assimilated from Portuguese Baroque, has astonished the world.

It was not so much the originality of the style that was evolved that led to its being hailed in various quarters as the birth of the new Brazilian architecture; it was rather the dashing spirit of the execution, the boldness of the young architects, and the favorable reception accorded by public opinion. A contributory cause came, perhaps, in the timely exhibition held at the Museum of Modern Art in New York, organized by Philip L. Goodwin and G. E. Kidder Smith in 1943.

The exhibition had a well-chosen title, 'Brazil Builds', and conveyed the impression that the whole country at that moment had become one vast building-site. The slogan 'a house a minute' became legendary throughout the world.

Brazil, then, assimilated the teaching of rational or functional (or whatever you like to call it) architecture that had been suspended in Europe on account of the war; or it may be more correct to say that she came up with a new interpretation of certain dogmas enunciated at the International Congress of Modern Architecture held in Athens in 1932, not bothering to go into them too deeply, avoiding the pious literalism which ·usually ends up by confusing or distorting the true creed, and, above all, adapting the rules to local conditions and to the requirements of a new aesthetic sense still inexistent but soon to become manifest. Nobody knew exactly what was wanted, yet it was felt that sheer enthusiasm would find the solution: no matter if there was wavering between different—even unorthodox—tendencies, too much reliance on improvisation, and an un-

conscious striving for rapid success; what was important was to experiment, to create an atmosphere, to act resourcefully.

The chances of politics also had an effect on the new movement. With the coming of the dictatorial government under Getulio Vargas in 1930 some intelligent minds gained influence in the administration. The innovators also succeeded in keeping the question clear of possible nationalistic objectors, who are always liable to make claims for tradition—even when there isn't any. The gleaming building of the Ministry of Education proclaims with astounding authority the end of the culturalistic period, which had culminated in an enormously expensive edifice in a pseudo-Gothic style in Rio, nicknamed the 'decayed tooth', now a joke tourist attraction on a par with the Maison du Monsieur Cheval. However, since the two conceptions of pompous culturalism and almost clinical rationalism were so far apart, a way had to be found to give the Ministry some elements a little more alluring than *brise-soleil* and glass. The solution adopted was to face the ground-floor walls with *azulejos* (ceramic panels) designed by Portinari, and to create a garden with tropical plants planned by the young Burle Marx.

The circumstances that enabled the Ministry to be built at all, by Lúcio Costa and his team of young architects according to Le Corbusier's general design, have already been related on an earlier page. A special recognition is, indeed, due to Costa. It was he who took over the Faculty of Architecture in Rio, overcame the opposition of the powerful groups with a vested interest in ugly urban architecture, and succeeded, with Warchavchik, in turning the Faculty's course in the direction of rationalism, which it has maintained ever since.

It is, therefore, to this group of architects, who favored the ideas of Le Corbusier, who enthusiastically attended his lectures in Rio, that we owe the first achievements of the new Brazilian architecture. Among them, Oscar Niemeyer became especially noted for his lively inventiveness and sense of plastic values, and his capacity not to quail before some particularly fantastic idea— a true heir of the Baroque masters in their taste for attracting attention, imposing their personality, and astonishing the beholder.

In the large cities, meanwhile, the exaggerated exploitation of the central areas inevitably led to the skyscraper, which was also favored by extensive adoption of the system by which the various tenements in a large building can have separate owners. In the last twenty years Rio (especially the Copacabana quarter), São Paulo, Recife, Pôrto Alegre, and Belo Horizonte have been changed out of all recognition by the numerous buildings of ten or more stories, which have even appeared in the outskirts. The smaller towns are doing their best to copy the big centers. Commercial architecture, still not subject to the discipline of properly regulated urban planning, has by now assumed the strictly functional pur-

171 Interior of G. Warchavchik's 'Modernist House' at São Paulo, 1931, which aroused so much controversy. The house was on show, and crowds of curious people came to see it. Study furniture designed by the architect. Sculpture: right, *Girl with Guitar* by V. Brecheret; on the desk, bronze by J. Lipchitz, *Guitarist*, now in the Museum of Art, São Paulo.

172 Opening-day of the Exhibition of the Modernist House.

173 The Modernist House.

174 Cover of the Exhibition catalogue.

175 F. L. Wright between L. Costa and G. Warchavchik at Rio de Janeiro in 1931, when he visited the city and observed the architecture of the young team, which he cordially praised.

176 Title of an article attacking the new architecture, *Ilustração Brasileira*, 1929.

171

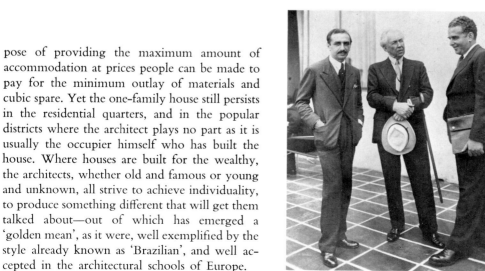

172

173

EXPOSIÇÃO DE UMA CASA MODERNISTA

POR GREGORI WARCHAVCHIK

RUA ITAPOLIS 119

174

pose of providing the maximum amount of accommodation at prices people can be made to pay for the minimum outlay of materials and cubic spare. Yet the one-family house still persists in the residential quarters, and in the popular districts where the architect plays no part as it is usually the occupier himself who has built the house. Where houses are built for the wealthy, the architects, whether old and famous or young and unknown, all strive to achieve individuality, to produce something different that will get them talked about—out of which has emerged a 'golden mean', as it were, well exemplified by the style already known as 'Brazilian', and well accepted in the architectural schools of Europe.

Ainda a ARCHITECTURA MODERNA

Dacio de Moraes ENGENHEIRO ARCHITECTO

Titolo d'un articolo polemico contro la nuova architettura, *Illustração Brasileira*, settembre '29.

175   176

177

178

179

180

The general tendency of architecture in the larger Brazilian cities between the two wars was one of hesitation and indecision; styles were imported from Europe which in Europe itself were already the subject of criticism and protest. The style of public buildings, which might have created some sort of a movement, was at the mercy of the individual taste of the clients, or of the impressions made on them by buildings they happened to have seen abroad. São Paulo, expanding at a tremendous pace both in population and industry, grew up without any city plan or urbanistic foresight and is unbelievably poor in boulevards and open spaces.

The gravity of this state of affairs was proclaimed by A. da R. Miranda in 1933 in the periodical *Base*. 'The building regulations', he wrote, 'are one of the biggest obstacles to the progress of architecture: strictly applied when they can stop anything good, liberally interpreted in favor of the bad. In matters of health and hygiene they will tolerate anything, land speculation is continually on the increase, the old farms are being divided up into minute lots, in each of which the building occupies 90 per cent of the area. There is no space for vegetation, and there is little air and light. At the opposite extreme, the authorities show no such laxity when they continually reject innumerable designs for lack of ornament on the façades. Their notion is that they are only concerned with aesthetics and form...'

But as for aesthetics—the only rule that was followed in the big cities was that of the general confusion created by the speculators. In vain did Warchavchik, Lúcio Costa, Rino Levi, and Alvaro Brazil attempt a counter-movement. During these years Brazil's

177 A. BRAZIL. Esther Building, São Paulo, 1936.
178 Matarazzo Industries Building, São Paulo, 1939, by the Italian architect Morpurgo.
179 A. BRAZIL. Plan of a floor of the Esther Building, with double-sized and minimum-sized apartments.
180 Cover of the periodical *Base*, 1933, edited by A. Altberg, which came out strongly on the side of those in favor of a renewal of Brazilian architecture.

181

182

183

184

largest industrial group, I. R. Matarazzo, built its central offices in São Paulo in 'Modernized Roman', the approved style of Mussolini's Rome, where the travertine was imported from, although there is some fine marble in Brazil. However, one fine building was erected at São Paulo by A. Brazil, with well-thought-out floor-plans, and this, together with two buildings by Rudofsky, served to show that the city was up-to-date in architecture.

Notwithstanding the short time he spent in Brazil, Rudofsky had considerable influence on modern architecture at São Paulo, and this was due to the houses here illustrated, which show both clarity of conception and understanding of tropical conditions. Unfortunately, people were still unprepared to accept the innovators that the fortunes of war were casting up on South American shores, and the only possible clients of these foreigners were other foreigners. It was only after the war, and especially owing to the influence of Le Corbusier, that the situation changed. Speaking of Rudofsky, Philip L. Goodwin wrote in *Brazil Builds*, 1943: 'Call it a house, pavilion, or pleasure dome of Xanadu, the Arnstein family has about as lovely a place to live in as could be found in the Americas. It is a splendid house... There is no such homogeneous and successful example of the modern house garden in the Americas.'

181 R. RUDOFSKY. Arnstein House, São Paulo, 1939. Model. Museum of Modern Art, New York.
182 Detail of the house itself.
183 R. RUDOFSKY. Frontini House, São Paulo, 1939. Isometric plan.
184 Front of the Frontini House.

185

186

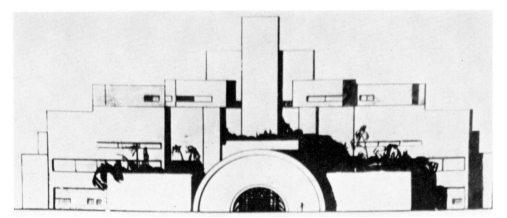

187

188

185 A. ALTBERG. Design for a house at Rio, 1934.

186 A. ALTBERG. Block of small apartment houses, Rio, 1934. Altberg was one of the innovators of Rio, and he organized the first Salon of Tropical Architecture, of which F. L. Wright was Honorary President, in 1933. The catalogue cited writings by W. Gropius and the Manifesto of the Athens Congress of 1932; G. Warchavchik, L. Costa, and E. H. Baumgart were named as pioneers.

187 F. DE CARVALHO. Design for State Government Palace, São Paulo, 1927.

188 F. DE CARVALHO. House at São Paulo, 1933, since demolished.

189 H. FEIJÓ. Model for a house at Recife, 1939, provided with a special system of cross-ventilation.

189

190

191

192

193

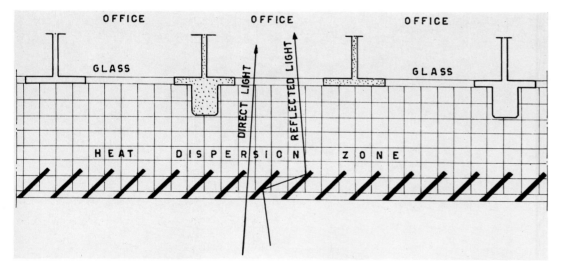

OFFICE   OFFICE   OFFICE

GLASS   DIRECT LIGHT   REFLECTED LIGHT   GLASS

HEAT   DISPERSION   ZONE

194

195

190 E. H. BAUMGART. Bridge over the Peixe river at Herval, state of Santa Catarina, 1929, built by canti-levering out from each end to the center. Central span, 68 m; minimum thickness, 1.70 m.

191 S. DE BRITO. Water-tower, Recife, 1937?

192 M. and M. ROBERTO. Perspective drawing of the winning design in the competition for the Brazilian Press Association (A.B.I.) Building in Rio, 1938.

193 The A.B.I. Building as constructed, 1938; it is still today the most outstanding example of the autonomy of the new Brazilian architecture, especially in the ingenious arrangement of the *brise-soleil*.

194 and 195 Plan and detail of the A.B.I. Building *brise-soleil*. The two Roberto brothers, joined later by their younger brother, Maurício, were the most important firm of architects in Rio, and their works aroused interest in the outer world as well. The firm is still active today under the sole and efficient guidance of Maurício. While on the subject of the *brise-soleil*, we may recall that Le Corbusier, in his city plan of Algiers, had carefully studied the requirements of climatic conditions analagous to those of the tropics, and during the months he spent in Brazil he advised that in new buildings the circulation of air and the

screening of the sun's rays should receive special attention. In fact, colonial architecture in Brazil already had traditional solutions to these problems, such as raising the height of doors and windows almost to that of the walls, the creation of cross-currents of air by careful placing of openings and balconies, and the use of *rotulas* (lattice-work shutters of Moorish origin introduced by the Portuguese) and partitions of semi-transparent matting.

196

198

199

196 Ministry of Education, Rio, nearly completed, about 1942. General design by Le Corbusier; actual design and execution by L. Costa, O. Niemeyer, J. Machado Moreira, C. Leão, E. Vasconcelos, and A. Reidy.
197 LE CORBUSIER. Page of a letter to P. M. Bardi, 1939, with observations on the planning of Rio.
198 and 199 Drawings by Le Corbusier, at an exhibition in Brazil, from the collection of L. Bardi, São Paulo.

200

201

202

Aspects of the Museum of Art, São Paulo, 1947.
200 General view of one of the rooms of the picture gallery.
201 Panel on Surrealism at a didactic exhibition.
202 The Cabinet of Form.

Founded by Assis Chateaubriand in 1947, the year which may be said to mark the completion of the clarification stage of Brazilian art, the Museum endowed the nation with the first and only picture gallery up to international standards in Latin America; it was conceived on didactic lines and organized to promote a knowledge of the history and problems of art, beginning with that of the national art, by means of a critical revaluation of the period now under discussion and with the presentation of the most important movements. Until 1950 it was possible to see in this picture gallery, as foreign critics were interested to note, works of Van Gogh, Cézanne, Mantegna, Matisse, and Picasso, side by side with paintings by the primitive artist José Antonio da Silva, a pioneer-type coffee-pot, ex-votos from the north-east, an Olivetti typewriter, and other useful objects—a 'Cabinet of Form' which anticipated the principles upon which this profile is based: to consider art as a whole, that is, and not in watertight compartments.

203 Foreign Office, Brasilia.

Brasilia and the new architecture

At the time of the city's inauguration, Brasilia was widely admired and praised, but was also, as in the case of any big success, the subject of criticism. On the basis of a city plan drawn up by Lúcio Costa, the winning entry in a competition that had attracted a large number of plans, each more rhetorical than the last, Oscar Niemeyer designed practically the entire capital and continues to superintend the work in progress, which is still far from completion. Lúcio Costa's plan is based on an idea that is practical and imaginative at the same time, midway between orthodox city planning, more preoccupied with measurements than with men, as laid down at congresses and in technical manuals, and the uncontrolled urbanization that has unfortunately been the curse of

the growing cities of Brazil. Costa's plan is an architect's rather than a sociologist's. All the usual buildings of a center of government are laid out, with an expenditure of space only possible in virgin territory, between the embracing arms of an artificial lake.

Niemeyer was given every freedom to develop his ideas, and he designed the Praça dos Tres Poderes, or 'Square of the Three Powers', with the same forcefulness that distinguished his earlier experiments in expanding the forms of Romanticized Baroque with a sense of plastic values approaching the sculptor's, and has in fact created what might almost be described as a work of sculpture containing within it an architectural system.

204 The first house to be built at Brasilia, prior to starting work on the city.
205 Cover of the catalogue of an exhibition on Brasilia held at the Museum of Decorative Arts, Paris, 1963, published by Éditions Forces-Vives.

206 During the building.
207–209 The form of the columns of the Palace of the Dawn becomes a widely diffused element of design.
210–212 Scenes from every-day life in Brasilia.
Photos by P. Scheier.

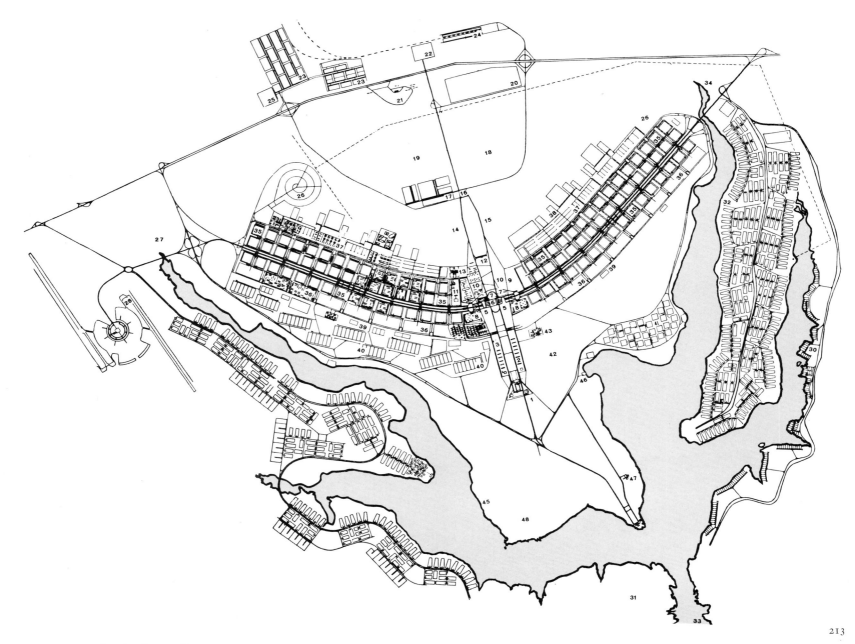

213 L. COSTA. Pilot plan for Brasilia, 1957.

1 Praça dos Tres Poderes
2 Avenue of the Ministries
3 Cathedral
4 Shopping Center
5 Cultural Center
6 Bus Station
7 Amusement Center
8 Banking Center
9 Commercial Center
10 Hotels
11 Hospital Center
12 Television Tower
13 Radio-Television Center
14 Sports Center
15 Jockey Club
16 Municipal Square

17 Press Center
18 Park
19 Meteorological Center
20 Residential
21 Low-priced residencies
22 Railway Station
23 Industrial Center
24 Warehouses
25 Station
26 Cemetery
27 Zoological Garden
28 Airport
29 Single-family houses
30 Single-family houses
31 Park
32 Single-family houses

33 Dam
34 Botanical Garden
35 Super-Quadra
36 Double Super-Quadra
37 Single-family houses
38 West development zone
39 East development zone
40 Embassies
41 Flats
42 University
43 Theater
44 Golf Club
45 Riding Club
46 Yacht Club
47 Tourist Hotel
48 Alvorada (the President's Palace of the Dawn)

214

215

216

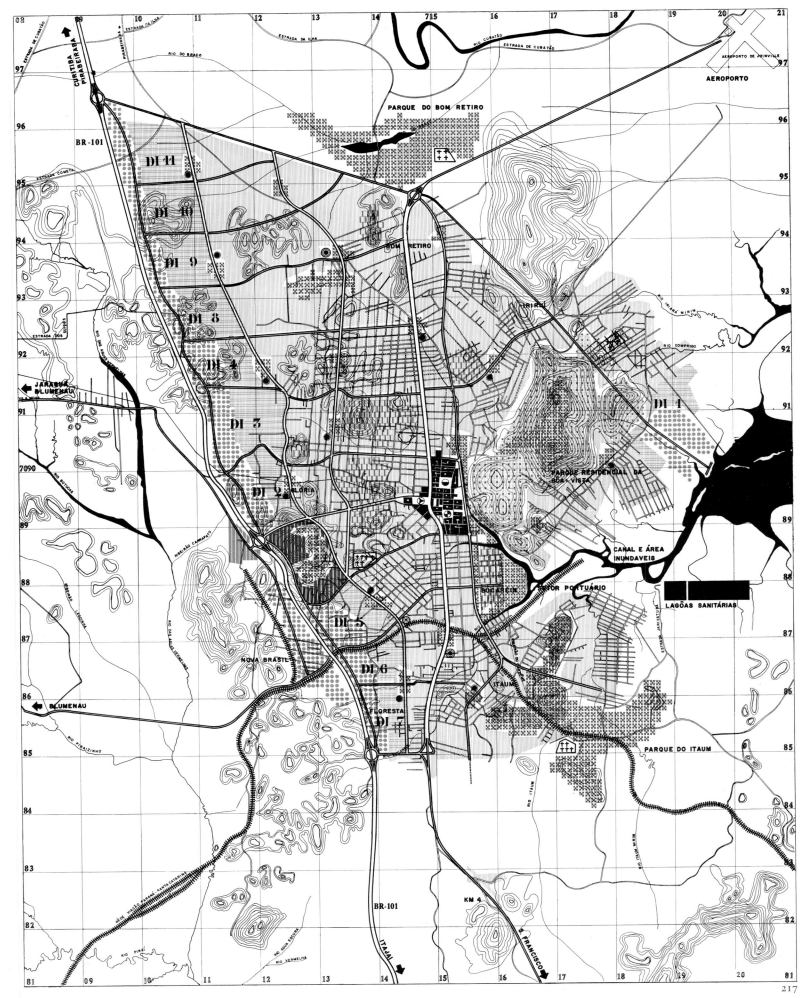

217

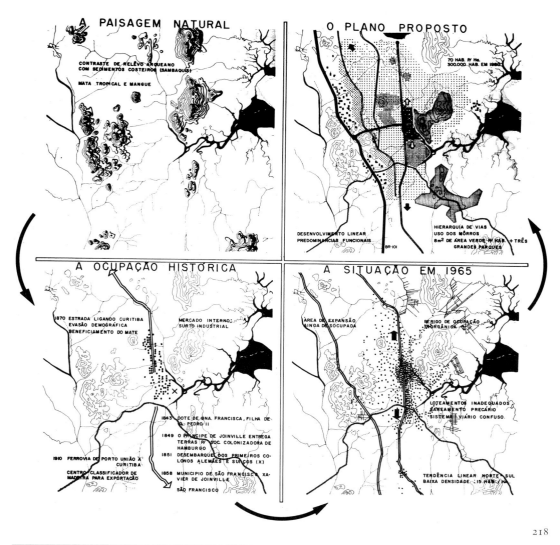

A PAISAGEM NATURAL

CONTRASTE DE RELEVO ARQUEANO
COM SEDIMENTOS COSTEIROS (SAMBAQUIS)

MATA TROPICAL E MANGUE

O PLANO PROPOSTO

70 HAB. P/ Ha.
300.000 HAB. EM 1980

DESENVOLVIMENTO LINEAR
PREDOMINÂNCIAS FUNCIONAIS

HIERARQUÍA DE VIAS
USO DOS MORROS
8m² DE ÁREA VERDE P/ HAB. + TRÊS
GRANDES PARQUES

BR-101

A OCUPAÇÃO HISTÓRICA

1870 ESTRADA LIGANDO CURITIBA
EVASÃO DEMOGRÁFICA
BENEFICIAMENTO DO MATE

MERCADO INTERNO:
SURTO INDUSTRIAL

1910 FERROVIA DE PORTO UNIÃO A
CURITIBA

CENTRO CLASSIFICADOR DE
MADEIRA PARA EXPORTAÇÃO

1843 DOTE DE ANA FRANCISCA, FILHA DE
D. PEDRO II

1849 O PRÍNCIPE DE JOINVILLE ENTREGA
TERRAS P/ SOC. COLONIZADORA DE
HAMBURGO

1851 DESEMBARQUE DOS PRIMEIROS CO-
LONOS ALEMÃES E SUÍÇOS (X)

1858 MUNICIPIO DE SÃO FRANCISCO XA-
VIER DE JOINVILLE

SÃO FRANCISCO

A SITUAÇÃO EM 1965

ÁREA DE EXPANSÃO
AINDA DESOCUPADA

PERIGO DE OCUPAÇÃO
INORGÂNICA

LOTEAMENTOS INADEQUADOS
SANEAMENTO PRECÁRIO
SISTEMA VIÁRIO CONFUSO.

TENDÊNCIA LINEAR NORTE SUL
BAIXA DENSIDADE: 15 HAB./ Ha.

218

219

220

217 Basic city plan for Joinville, 1965: use of land (zoning). Planning director, Architect Jorge Wilheim; assistant, Paulo Zimbres; social and economic research, Sociedade Serete; sociological consultant, Octávio Ianni; legal consultants, H. L. Meirelles and B. R. Moraes; landscaping, Rosa Grena Kliass; symbol, Architect A. Sanovicz.

Predominantly residential zones: 100 inhab. per hectare (2.471 acres)
Industrial workers' residential zones: 200 inhab. per hectare
Special residential zones: 300–350 inhab. per hectare
Residential park: minimum lot 2,000 sq.m. (about ½ acre)

Educational zone	green vertical stripes
Parks and gardens	green
Industrial zones	violet dots
Central food market	blue dot
Predominantly commercial zone	black squares
New railway station	⊕
Civic center and theater	◐
Model shopping center	◒
Bus station	⊖
Neighborhood centers and food markets	●
Future secondary centers	◉

218 The elements of the problem, or how to find, at a new level and in modern terms, integration with the natural landscape. The immediate danger was the absence of any organic development and the consequent threat of overcrowding.

219 View of the city, showing factories mixed up with houses. At the center, the spot where the principal access road from the motorway meets the north-south axis, and where it is proposed to locate the bus station.

220 This row of royal palms (*Roystonea oleracea*) will be amplified to make a 'palm forum' adjoining the new civic center, planned for the square where German influence in the architecture is still evident.

City planning in Brazil in the last twenty years has by no means kept abreast of architecture. Cities expanded at a tremendous rate and in utter confusion, due to the pressing need for housing and the consequent opportunities for speculation. An occasional attempt at order was made: in 1935 A. Corrêa Lima planned Goiânia in accordance with French theories; other interesting plans were never put into effect. But after the example of Brasilia, which in this field, too, marks the beginning of a new era, young architects are turning their attention to urban planning. To appreciate the importance of this new movement, we may take a brief glance at the basic plan for Joinville, S.C. The town is situated in a valley, near a river, has a damp and unprepossessing climate, and the surrounding country is hilly and partly covered with tropical vegetation. It has certain distinctive features due to German and Swiss emigration dating back to a 'Hamburgian Colonial Society' of 1849, and was practically isolated—also linguistically—from the rest of Brazil. The present population of 90,000, at a density of 15 inhabitants per hectare (about 6 per acre), is increasing at 6 per cent per annum, and is estimated to reach 650,000 by the end of the century. The economy was based on the production of mate until about 1930, subsequently timber. Inter-city traffic passes right through the town and encounters cross-traffic in the middle of the commercial and industrial center. There is a deficiency of civic buildings and services, and a lack of informal centers of informal meetings that might help to promote a sense of civic responsibility, which is not in itself wanting, nor is a capacity for commercial enterprise. In short, a town eminently suitable for radical re-planning. Architect Jorge Wilheim, who was in charge of the general direction of the plan, is a great believer in progressive principles and legislation tending to dynamic solutions in the social and economic sense. Having studied the site, he has indicated reclamation as the first task to be undertaken, followed by measures for an urban plan designed to maintain a balance between the town and the natural features of hills and river, indicating some of the hills for the siting of blocks of flats. This integration between landscape and building is the most vital aspect of the plan, and is in accordance with Brazilian urban-planning theories which, while tracing their origins to the precepts of the Athens Chart, seek to adapt themselves to underdeveloped conditions. The Joinville plan provided for 8 sq.m. of park and garden per inhabitant (São Paulo at present has only 1 sq.m. per inhabitant); there will be a continuous park along the river, with recreation centers, and other parks are planned in the surroundings. The main elements of the plan are its linear character and the clear distinctions between the civic, commercial, and cultural centers, and a not too rigid zoning, adapted to Brazilian conditions and allowing for expansion and the benefits of public services. Since the whole of Brazil is in need of regional and urban renewal, it is easy to see the task that awaits the generation now graduating from the Faculties of Architecture, which have finally begun to teach urban planning.

221

222

223

224

225

226

227

228

229

230

In these pages we shall see something of what has now become a familar scene in Brazil's progress towards the conquest of the 'new frontier'. The whole of the Amazon basin will one day become a productive region containing all kinds of enterprises. A start has already been made in the Amapá Territory, at a point in the forest more than 100 miles from the Amazon. The discovery of exceptional deposits of manganese has entirely transformed the region: mining plants have been built, as well as two towns, Vila Serra do Navio, the mining center, and Vila Amazonas, the port, and a railway between them. The questions of planning and architecture posed some interesting problems: it was not merely a matter of supplying the practical means of existence, but of adapting to a new social environment the workpeople recruited in the district and who had hitherto led a precarious existence in the wet climate (seven months a year of great rains), exposed to malaria and all the adversity of the Amazon forest. The two towns have been planned for an eventual population of 25,000. Architect, O. Bratke.

221 and 222 The environment.
223 Houses of local inhabitants before the discovery of the deposits.
224 Virgin forest at the point where Vila Serra do Navio now stands.
225 Partial view of Vila Amazonas.
226 The Juscelino Kubitschek Bridge on the Tocantins river, Brasilia-Belém motorway, designed by Sérgio Marques de Souza.

227 Another house of local inhabitants before the coming of the new town.
228 System for screening off sunlight and allowing ventilation in one of the new houses.
229 Partial view of Vila Serra do Navio.
230 Houses for management staff of the ICOMI company, holders of the mining concession.

231

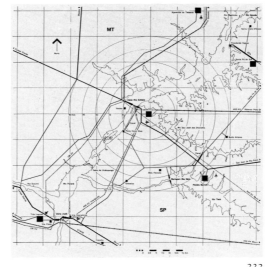

232

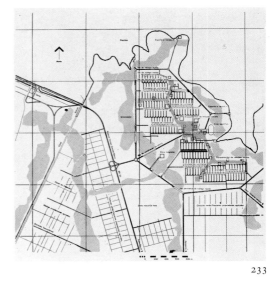

233

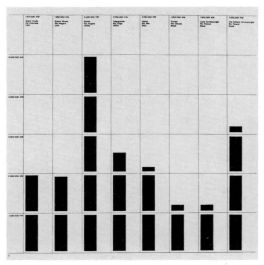

234

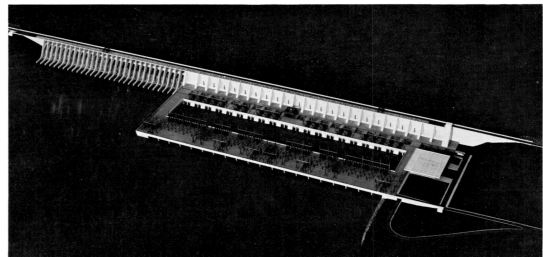

235

The hydro-electric scheme at Urubupungá, on the Paraná river, which exploits the enormous water-power potential of the Paraná basin, an area of 180,000 square miles, comprises the two dams and generating stations at Jupiá and Ilha Solteira. When completed it will be the second largest hydro-electric complex in the world, with a power potential of 4,400 megawatts and an annual production of 26,000,000 megawatt-hours. Undertaken by the Celusa company, with the aid of the Federal Government and the Governments of the States interested, at a cost of $900m., it is one of the biggest enterprises of industrial architecture in Brazil—and of urban planning, since it also involved the provision, at each of the stations, of a temporary urban nucleus for the construction workers, and a permanent one for the operating staff. At Jupiá, completed in 1966, 2,300,000 cubic yards of rock were

excavated for the generating station, and 6,250,000 cubic yards of earth were moved in the construction of the dam, in which 5,000 metric tons of steel were used. Power potential 1,200 megawatts. The station at Ilha Solteira will be producing 3,200 megawatts from 1962. General project by the Società Edison, Milan; working plans by Themag Engehnaria, São Paulo; architecture and urban planning by E. R. Carvalho Mange and Ariaki Kato.

231 Hydro-electric stations in the Paraná basin, the main sources of power for central and southern Brazil.
232 Map showing the two dams.
233 Projected urban nucleus for the Ilha Solteira station.
234 Chart of the world's leading hydro-electric stations.
235 Model of the Ilha Solteira dam.

236 The Jupiá dam and generating station.
237 Temporary urban nucleus for 12,000 workers, recruited from all over Brazil, and their families, including public services installations, a school for 2,000 pupils, hotels, church, amusement centers.
238 Projected urban nucleus for the operating staff of the Jupiá station: 1,200 inhabitants.
239 The temporary Jupiá nucleus seen from the air.

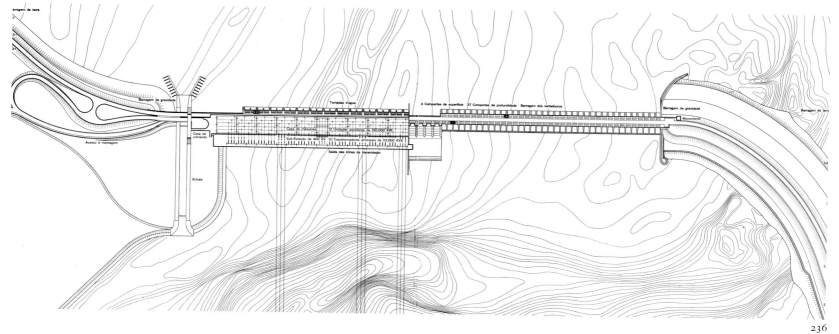

236

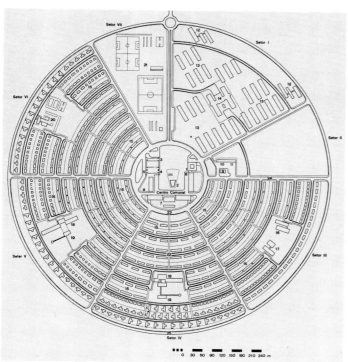

237

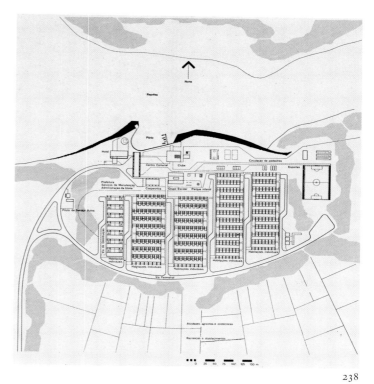

238

239

240 The Museum of Art, São Paulo; the building is in prestressed concrete. Photo by E. Keffel.

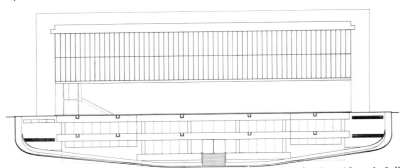

241 Front elevation of the Museum and the Belvedere, facing the Avenida 9 de Julho.

242 L. BO. Projected museum at São Vicente, 1951. The structural idea of the present São Paulo Museum of Art derives from this project, which was never carried out.

243 Sketch-plan of the Belvedere terrace.

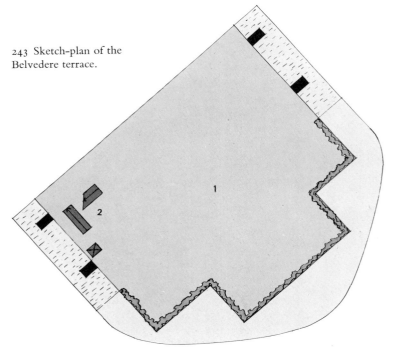

244 Sketch-plan of the Civic Hall and auditoriums.

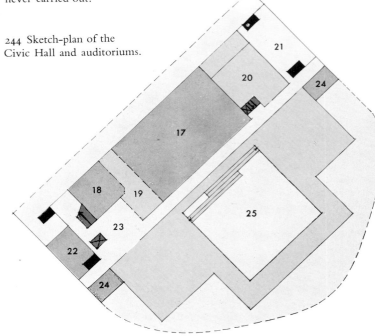

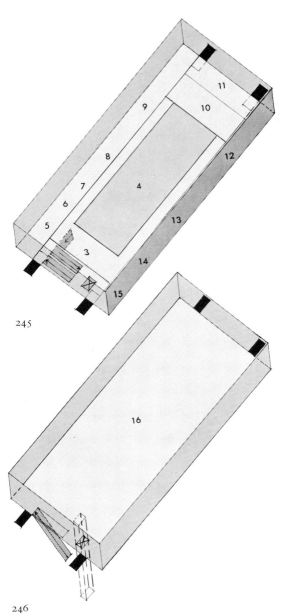

245

247

246

At the Belvedere of the Trianon, a popular center in São Paulo, the Museum of Art building, designed by the architect Lina Bo, is nearing completion. The condition imposed by the city authorities that the open space of the Belvedere should be entirely unencumbered by supporting structures forced the architect to adopt a self-contained design and to use prestressed concrete. The building, which is suspended over the Belvedere, has a clear span of 246 feet. The structure consists essentially of four pilasters and two pairs of beams of prestressed concrete, one pair below the other. The floor of the picture gallery rests on the lower pair of beams. The upper pair ride over the top of the roof and from them the upper floor, containing the Museum offices and the room for temporary exhibitions, is suspended by steel cables. The great terrace of the Belvedere is itself the roof of a large Civic Hall designed for cultural and political assemblies.

The Belvedere, surrounded by plants and flower borders, will act as a public garden and as a place for out-of-door exhibitions, receptions, and concerts. The whole architectural complex is, in its extreme simplicity, consciously intended an an exercise in rationalism. Technical collaborator for prestressed concrete and structural calculations, Engineer José Carlos de Figueiredo Ferraz and Associates.

245 Sketch-plan of the Museum offices and room for temporary exhibitions.
246 Sketch-plan of the picture gallery.
247 Sketch for open-air exhibitions on the Belvedere terrace.
248 There will be no walls or panels in the picture gallery; the paintings, with plain uniform list-frames, will be fixed to sheets of toughened glass.
249 Information cards, with notes on the artist and his work, will be fixed on the back of each picture.

248

249

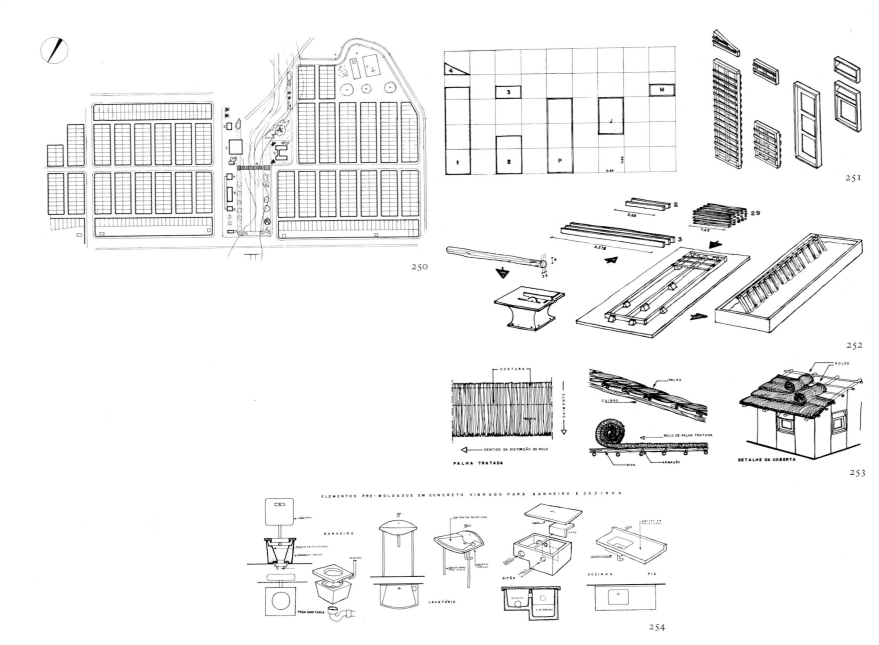

250

251

252

253

254

A. G. BORSOI. Ultra low-cost housing scheme at Cajueiro Seco, Pernambuco, 1965. Social welfare project for improving the *mocambos*, dwellings of a primordial type made of daub reinforced with wood and still being built in remote parts of Brazil. The architect, having studied the manual aptitudes of a group of farm laborers and their families, has rationalized the work so as to achieve the minimum of waste in the utilization of timber and to require no equipment on the site more elaborate than a circular saw. Logs are sawn into strips of the required lengths and thicknesses, and these are made up into four standard types of frames on special work benches fitted with guide-blocks. The frames, after impregnation with a preservative, are then assembled into houses of various sizes. The composition of the daub and the method of its application have also been improved. The thatch is pre-fabricated in standard-length rolls which can be easily laid out on the rafters. Finally, sanitary and kitchen equipment, hitherto lacking in such houses, has been provided. The result —which is not to be regarded as more than a temporary solution even in low cost building—is an improvement in the living conditions of the group and a considerable saving in expenditure.

250 General plan of the scheme: 1 houses, 2 chapel, 3 assembly hall, 4 shop, 5 and 6 workshops, 7 dispensary, 8 shelter, 9 school.
251 Construction elements: 1–4, frames, P door, J large window, M small window.
252 Production line for frames.
253 Thatch in pre-sewn rolls.
254 Sanitary and kitchen fixtures in vibrated concrete.

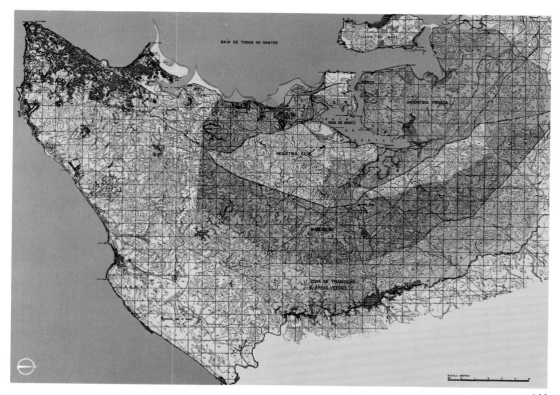

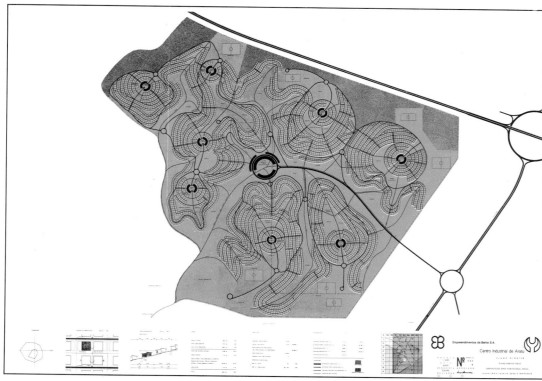

255 Industrial Center of Aratú, Bahia state, undertaken by the Empreendimentos da Bahia company;
architect, Sérgio Bernardes. The center occupies a
large area on the Bay of Todos os Santos, and consists
of a port zone (orange), 3,200 acres; a heavy industrial
zone (violet), 10,000 acres; a light industrial zone
(pink), 8,200 acres; a residential and commercial zone
(brown), 21,800 acres; and a green-belt zone (green),
22,200 acres. In the whole area there are 42,000 acres
of public open spaces and non-built-up areas.
256 Plan of the first housing estate center, which is to
be built on co-operative lines.
257 Scheme for industrial housing units with allowance for extensions; the broken lines show the sewage
network.
258 Section, showing how the houses, built on sloping
land, are arranged to have a clear view of the sea.

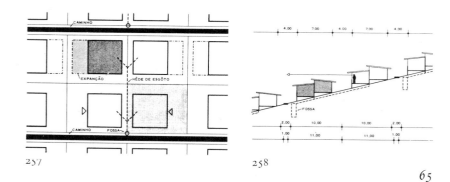

259

260

261

262

Pianta cy Rino Levi

263

259 S. BERNARDES. House of Sr. João Souza Dantas, 1965, São Paulo.

260 J. V. ARTIGAS. Stadium of the São Paulo Football Club, 1961. Detail of the vestibule.

261 MARCELO ROBERTO, H. UCHÔA, S. BERNARDES, MAURÍCIO ROBERTO. Model of a group of buildings at Rio.

262 A. E. REIDY. Project for a students' theater.

263 R. LEVI. The architect's house at São Paulo, the whole of which, furniture included, was conceived and designed at the same time with the result that all the elements combined to produce an architectural unity that at the time of its construction, in 1944, was an early example of integration with natural surroundings. Plan: 1 vestibule, 2 toilet, 3 living-room, 4 veranda, 5 dining-room, 6 living-room patio, 7 bedrooms, 8 dressing-rooms, 9 bathrooms, 10 bathrooms patio, 11 offices, 12 kitchen, 13 larder, 14 refuse, 15 kitchen patio, 16 garage, 17 storehouse, 18 washhouse, 19 children's playroom, 20 front garden.

264 View of the main entrance.

264

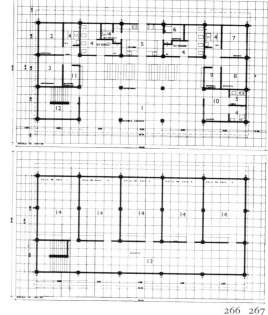

265

266 267

269

270

268

265–268 F. BOLONHA. The Joseph Bloch Elementary
School, Rio, 1966.
266 Ground-floor plan: 1 playground, 2 Principal's
study, 3 teachers' room, 4 lavatories, 5 kitchens,
6 larder, 7 surgery, 8 dental surgery, 9 cleaning
materials, 10 janitor, 11 educational materials, 12 stairs.
267 Upper-floor plan: 13 corridor, 14 classrooms.
268 Classroom interior: overhead lighting and open-
ended roof ventilation.
269 F. BOLONHA. The André Maurois State College,
Rio, 1966.
270 Classroom interior of the same: lighting through
sun-shutters.
271 F. BOLONHA. The Roma School, Rio, 1966.

271

272

273

274

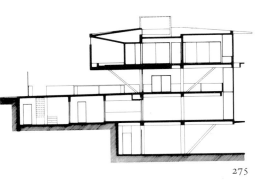

275

276

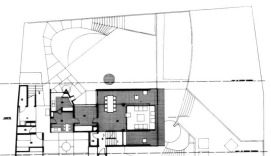

277

278

The younger Brazilian architects are keenly interested in experimental forms and delight in designing unconventional and fantastic buildings, especially single-family houses. Here are two examples.

272 and 273 J. GUEDES. House at São Paulo, 1961.
274 View of the living-room.
275 Sectional plan.
276 Garden and swimming-pool.
277 First-floor plan.
278 Top-floor plan.
279 and 280 E. LONGO. House at Guarujá, Santos, 1967.
281, 282 and 283 Views of the living-room.

279

280

281

282

283

284

285

284 J. MACHADO MOREIRA and associated architects. University City, Rio de Janeiro, 1956, built on an artificial island of 1,380 acres created by filling in the space between nine islets in Guanabara Bay and linked with the mainland and with Ilha do Governador by three bridges. Planned for 30,000 students.
285 Plan of University City, Rio: 1 Institute of Puericulture, 2 Hospital and Clinics, 3 Engineering School, 4 Faculty of Architecture, 5 Printing Office.
286 Faculty of Architecture, University City, Rio.
287 Institute of Puericulture, University City, Rio.
288 J. MACHADO MOREIRA. Private house, Rio, 1958.

286

287

288

69

289

290

291

292

293

294

295

296

297

289 R. OHTAKE. House at São Paulo, 1966.

290 T. CRISTOFANI. Façade of a restaurant, São Paulo, 1966.

291 H. MINDLIN and associated architects. Guanabara State Bank, Rio, 1966.

292 J. W. TOSCANO. House at São Paulo, 1965.

293 and 294 R.´B. LEFÈVRE and S. FERRO. Houses at São Paulo, 1966.

295 S. DE BRITO. House at Asunción, Paraguay, 1966.

296 and 297 E. SILVEIRA MELLO. Bank branch (can be taken down and re-erected), São Paulo, 1965.

298

299

300

298 J. RUCHTI. Hall of the Banco Federal Itaú-Sulamericano, São Paulo, 1967.

299 and 300 J. ZALSZUPIN and R. CRUZ. L'Atelier shop, Rio, 1965.

301 I. RUCHTI. Terrace garden on the top floor of a building at Rio, 1967.

302 R. BURLE MARX. Garden at Petrópolis, state of Rio. This artist's activities in the field of garden design, which can become at times, in Brazil, indistinguishable from architecture, are well known. The luxuriance and prodigality of nature offers almost unlimited possibilities to the architect, and Burle Marx, as has been shown in a book specially devoted to him (P. M. Bardi, *The Tropical Gardens of Burle Marx*, Amsterdam-Rio de Janeiro, Colibris, 1964), has taken advantage of them with imagination and rare botanical sensibility.

303 F. LEIRNER. *Sculpture*, 1966, in a garden at Campos de Jordão, state of São Paulo. Photo by João Xavier.

Sculpture

Sculpture has a tradition in Brazil, but it has almost always, as an adjunct to architecture or in the making of sacred images, been involved with the Baroque of the Portuguese motherland. The most famous figure in this tradition is Aleijadinho, who was active for some fifty years from about 1760, and whose case is so well known as to require no further comment. After the end of the colonial period sculpture was imported, and so were the sculptors, who established mason's yards and foundries to supply the demand for funerary sculpture and public monuments. The prevailing style was outdated academic.

Exceptions, with any sense of contemporaneity, are rare. In the chapter on the approach to modernity we have seen something of the work of Brecheret, and of Maria Martins, who is still active and up to date. An isolated case was that of Flávio de Carvalho, though he produced few sculptural works. In these years the most original sculpture came from Lasar Segall. After the Second World War some of these sculptors continued to be active but produced nothing particularly outstanding. It is only in the last ten years, especially with the arrival of some young foreign artists, that sculpture has been showing signs of branching out in various directions in pursuit of modern forms. As in the case of painting, this usually amounts to imitating foreign trends. In any case, the state of sculpture in Brazil is not represented by the works to be seen in the new capital which, as may have been guessed, suffer from lack of coordination between the architecture and the other arts. Sculptors are still few. Demand is limited to decoration, or to the public monument, which is always commissioned from some academic statuary. Examples of monuments by sculptors who have not adjusted to bourgeois taste are rare.

304

305

306

307

304 A. DA HORA. *Hiroshima*, 1958. Polished concrete, heigt 90 cm. Private collection, São Paulo.

305 A. DA HORA. *Motherhood*, 1965. Polished plaster of Paris, height 100 cm. Collection: Mirante das Artes, São Paulo.

306 A. DOS SANTOS. *Motherhood*, 1958. Wood, height 70 cm. Collection: Mirante das Artes, São Paulo.

307 A. DENIS. *Indian Girl of Brazil*, 1956. Bronze, heigt 175 cm. Collection: Heuberger, São Paulo.

308 A. DOS SANTOS. *Figure*, 1962. Wood, height 36 cm. Private collection, São Paulo.

309 V. PRADO. Model for a Monument to Villa-Lobos, to be executed in pink granite, length 380 cm., for the Municipal Auditorium of Pôrto Alegre.

309

308

Images of designs by the so-called visual operators, who today possess the field, are nowadays immediately launched into space and bounced back to every part of the globe by means of artificial satellites. The transmissions follow and cross each other with such rapidity that the images pile up into an amorphous mass in which their original raisons d'être are completely lost, and give rise to new terminologies in which the word *art*, if it occurs at all, seems particularly out of place. There was a time when such battles could only be won by the whole weight of the forces deployed; today the avant-gardes can win them by themselves. They no sooner appear in the field than they are welcomed with hosannas and the victory is theirs; all the nations bow down to the victors, accept their conditions, and spread their doctrines throughout the world—until a new avant-garde comes along.

One can safely say, as a matter of mere observation, and without any ulterior motive, that one only needs to glance at any international exhibition to realize that if, by some chance, all the labels of the participating nations were put on the wrong rooms, it would certainly not be the public who would notice anything wrong: the international character of contemporary art is an obvious fact. Many critics exert themselves to discover national roots and traditions in certain artists, a task that often involves them in the most fantastic contortions. At all events, for the great number of plastic artists who are responsible for the bulk of ever-increasing production, it seems to me that 'international' is the term to be used, as it has been used by art historians in referring to types of Gothic or Baroque that adopted common elements purged of local characteristics and evolved generic forms that might be valid anywhere. In those days the world was small and sparsely populated; people's thoughts and actions obeyed a single aesthetic order, a single religion, and a semi-ancestral hierarchy. Nowadays all sorts of romantic styles flourish and multiply daily —esoteric, ironic, abstruse, inaccessible, contradictory. They create only uncertainty and confusion, and the possibility of explaining them to the masses is highly problematical, and is made still more difficult by social and political interferences, the confusion of progress, and philosophic doubts. Yet one hears it said that culture is on the point of being transferred from the ivory towers to the masses, ready to give up its haughty

310

311

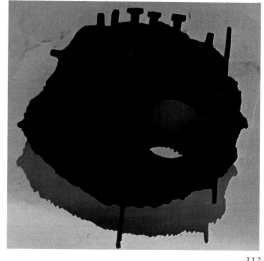

312

313

310 N. VLAVIANOS. *Group of sculptures*, 1966. Iron painted with nitrocellulose lacquer, each 160 cm. high. Collection of the artist.
311 CACIPORÉ TORRES, *The Distant Mountain*, 1965. Cast iron, height 160 cm. Collection of the artist.
312 CACIPORÉ TORRES. *Vibration 1000*, 1965. Bronze, height 47 cm. Collection of the artist.
313 CACIPORÉ TORRES. *Vibration IV*, 1965. Cast iron, height 70 cm. Collection: Saul Libman, São Paulo.

314

315

tone and become less exclusive. The fact is that the problem of culture today is that of the divorce, with no prospects of reconciliation, between the production of the artist, on the one hand, and the capacity or desire of the consumer to understand it, on the other—as, indeed, many students of 'communication' have noted, though they often complicate the problem.

It was inevitable that the international style should arrive in Brazil, with all its complicated organization into departments and sub-departments, all its manifestoes, tendencies, and secessions, all its proselytes and publicizers of the latest fads,

themselves understood only by small groups of initiates. And it is not for the first time, as we have seen, that ready-made philosophies have arrived from overseas. The nation has become what it is by dint of importing them. Originally it was the doctrine of the Church, later to be strongly attacked by Positivism, followed more recently by a weak Neo-Thomist reaction. Romanticism had the best of welcomes, the more so in that it encountered a disposition to melancholy typical of the tropics, a tendency to indulge in nostalgic memories of the past, a liking for twilight tones, pathetic music, and 'fragments';

in its various aspects it had many followers—until the arrival of the counter-attraction in the form of Modernism (which, it should be made clear, had no connexion of the movement of the same name in Spain and Italy).

Modernism was to have brought about a renaissance. But a generation later one could still read such comments as one made by Sacheverell Sitwell in the preface to the catalogue of an exhibition of as many as seventy Brazilian artists held at Burlington House in 1944, to the effect that Brazilian painters were still under the influence of second-rate foreign artists, and that it would be

314 H. RODRIGUES. *Mural*, 1965, at the Hotel Ferrareto, Guarujá, Santos. Bricks, cement, coloring matter, 3.40 × 27 m.
315 L. WOOLF. *Sculpture*, 1965. Bronze, height 37 cm. Collection: E. Wolf, São Paulo.
316 T. SHIMITZU *Sculpture*, 1966. Concrete, height, 60 cm. Collection of the artist.
317 E. HERING. *Homus*, 1965. Bronze, height 60 cm. Collection: Giorgio Moroni. São Paulo.

316

317

advisable that a French or English master should be asked to go out and save the situation—from which it appears that the road to independence is long and difficult, especially in these days of so much international intercourse.

Now, more than twenty years later, the situation has improved. Not that any startlingly new philosophies have been invented, but a robust group of Brazilian artists has appeared in the workshops where the latest international innovations are manipulated, and have brought contributions worthy of mention. The Brazilians who belong to the Paris School have been noted by critics for the brilliance and seriousness of their work, which has created much the same impression when shown in international exhibitions or in national exhibitions in other countries. No critic dare say nowadays that Brazil could do with foreign art masters. In fact, numerous Brazilians themselves now teach in schools of international repute, and they are much in demand on account of their creative and teaching abilities.

Apart from architecture, which has been receiving favorable consideration for some time, painting and engraving are now also beginning to create a good impression. The same may be said of some of the younger generation of sculptors, who are responsible for the first flowering—in its most difficult form, the figurative—of this hitherto little-practised art.

At this point it comes natural to ask: What are the reactions, among critics and the public, to all these activities of Brazilian artists, whose ideas and work I have so far mentioned only with the impartiality of a general survey?

An examination of critical reactions, now that the participation of Brazilian art in the 'international style' has become a fact, shows that criticism (not to mention names for the moment), no less than art, conforms to fashion. The artist's product is accepted or rejected without any attempt to find in it spiritual messages, presages of beatific or infernal destinies, and still less the 'alienation' one now hears so much talk about. Actual choice in Brazil is restricted to those who buy works of art or give commissions for buildings—which is a very restricted circle when one thinks of the masses of people, in town or country, who are, in fact, the consumers.

The well-to-do classes who purchase works of art look for guidance in their choice to the press, which is very influential in this field. A newspaper can promote a new artist overnight. The introduction of good modern architecture from

318

319

320

318 F. STOCKINGER. *Amazon*, 1965. Bronze, height 178 cm. Collection of the artist.
319 F. STOCKINGER. *Sentinel of the Cave*, 1966. Wood and iron, height 180 cm. Collection of the artist.
320 F. STOCKINGER. *Amazon*, 1967. Wood and metal, 200 × 150 cm. Collection: Dr. Edmundo Freitas, São Paulo.

321

322

321 L. MILLER. *Astrolabe*, 1965. Bronze, height 120 cm. Collection of the artist.
322 S. ELBING. *The Sea*, 1962. Polychrome concrete, height 70 cm. Collection of the artist.
323 M. CRAVO. *Polyvalent Winged Creature*, 1960. Iron, height 260 cm. Collection of the artist.
324 C. BLANC. *Sculpture of Planes*, 1965. Iron, height 175 cm. Collection of the artist.

323

324

abroad, and its being accepted, were due to the influence of journalism, especially to the repercussions of the 'Brazil Builds' exhibition held at the Museum of Modern Art in New York in 1943. Its favorable reception was flattering to the national self-esteem, which is always ready to enjoy foreign praise. Other examples are the cases of Manabu Mabe, who got no fame from his award at the Fifth Biennial of São Paulo, but did from that of the First Paris Biennial a year later, and Wesley Lee, always rejected by the Brazilian biennials, but famous the day he received a cable announcing an award from the Biennial of Tokyo.

These facts are symptomatic and indicate the decisive effect of foreign opinion. The phenomenon is not exclusively Brazilian. In Europe, too, and, in fact, throughout the world, the judgements of foreigners are looked upon as if they were judgements of posterity, already a part of history—as Leopardi was the first to remark. The United States engaged in chicanery in order that Rauschenberg might receive the Venice award: diplomacy had played its part with as much zeal as it puts into winning a cold war. The politics of awards, a by-product of international politics, has its importance, and its effect on the nation's art. Prizes are given, in ever increasing numbers, for all sorts of specialties—anything to attract attention, as if it were bathing beaches or industrial products that were being advertised—in the form of money or medals or tin-pot trophies, until there is not an artist who cannot boast of one, like a champion boxer or cyclist.

It is the fact of all this prize-giving, and the attempt to keep up with the latest fashion (which is what the juries go by), that must be borne in mind in considering Brazilian art. The newest trends immediately find their publicists and press-agents who put them over on the public and force the artists to conform to them. No sooner does the announcement go forth of the existence of action painting, of Pop art, or of Op art, though it may cross the ocean with the velocity of a jet (losing, incidentally, in the equatorial clouds Pollock's provocative and angry tenseness, the irony of the New Yorker's reaction to cybernetics, and some of those parallel lines that seem to have been put into Op painting for the sole purpose of scarifying the beholder's eye), than it finds a group of artists all ready waiting to take up the new creed. This is what happened in the case of Concretism, when certain young artists who had been giving unrestrained vent to explosive bursts of expression calmly got down to painting with ruler, compass, set square, and slide rule. Now one hears no more of the group, but its adepts may be discovered busily turning out work according to the newest fashions.

Every time one of these little bombshells bursts over Brazil one is hard put to it to explain that action painting, for instance, might have been something new in the eighteenth century, when it was used in bookbinding for the abstract

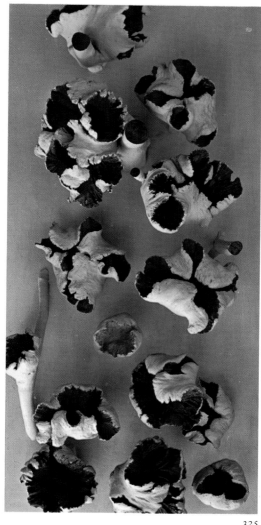

325

326

325 KRAJCBERG. *Flowers of Wood*, 1965. Wood, 160 × 75 cm. Collection: Georges Lafond, Paris.
326 KRAJCBERG. *Flower of Wood*, 1966. Wood, 75 × 75 cm. Collection of the artist.
It would seem that Krajcberg had studied the appearance of the lunar crust and re-created the formations, volcanoes, depressions that astral photography reveals —or that his is the task of an artist who makes real to us what we see in dreams.

327 F. WEISSMANN. *Sculpture*, 1965. Hammered galvanized sheet, height 80 cm. Collection of the artist.
328 F. WEISSMANN. *Sculpture*, 1965. Scrap metal pressed and colored, height 90 cm. Collection of the artist.

328   327

329 C. G. TENIUS. *Manifestation II*, 1964. Welded iron, height 34 cm. Collection of the artist.
330 M. SALGUEIRO. *Sculpture III*, 1964. Welded iron with sound elements, height 70 cm. Collection: Pan American Union, Washington, D.C.
331 J. A. PEDROSA. *Sculpture*, 1953. Bronze, height 25 cm. Collection of the artist.

329

331

330

sprinkling of endpapers and edges, that pictures made with garbage, or with bits of bone, or collages, had become a bore after the second Dadaism and the third Futurism, that Op art is a rehash of seventeenth-century geometrical designs, and so on.

The manufacturer of art has no sense of history, for if he had had any—and it is strange that he has never thought of it—he might have found ready to hand unexploited resources in Brazilian archeology, a mine of formal elements no less

productive than that of Negro art; instead, he is content to re-elaborate what has already been re-elaborated.

That there has still been no real attempt to rethink the whole question of the nation's art is borne out by comments on the present state of affairs by some of the younger critics. Ferreira Goular writes: 'All the changes of tendency [in Brazilian painting] are imposed from outside, in line with the mutations that take place in Paris and New York... with the result that none of them can be

experienced in depth.' And J. G. Merquior: 'What is now, in our country, expected of the artist is that he should be responsible, that he should look upon objective problems of our own society realistically... The Brazilian artist is asked to accept social responsibility, or, in other words, to help to establish a concrete vision of the world that surrounds him, but the undertaking he is asked to give goes no further than this.' Finally, Leandro Konder asks: 'Must our poetry, to reach a high artistic standard, restrict its audience to an

332

333

334

332 S. DE CAMARGO. *Modulated Tower*, 1966. Carrara marble, height 330 cm. Collection of the artist.

333 S. DE CAMARGO. *Relief rayonnant No. 2/21*, 1964. Painted wood, height 35 cm. Collection: Gromholt, Oslo.

334 S. DE CAMARGO. Double-faced wall, 1966. Auditorium of the Foreign Ministry, Brasilia; architect, O. Niemeyer.

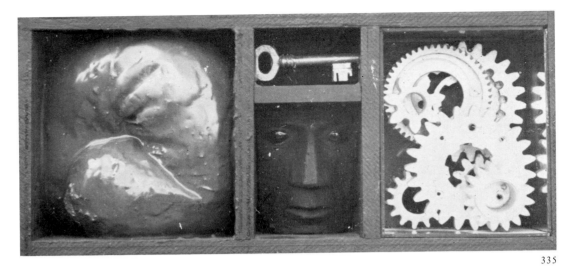

ever shrinking number of specialists? What, finally, will be the real possibilities of effective cultural expressiveness open to our painters in face of the dictates of fashion imposed throughout the globe by the international art merchants? Rejecting, on principle, the futile idea of cultural isolation, what standards must we be guided by, in assimilating the influence of foreign cultures, if we are not to ignore the deepest needs of our own people?'

These are problems to which the younger generation, people still in their twenties, are giving much anxious thought; and it will be among those of them who survive the coming crisis that the representatives of the art, which, circumstances permitting, will bear the banner of Brazil in the international arena, will be found.

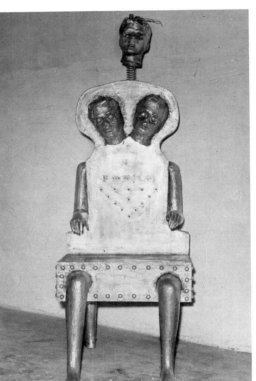

In Brazil, as elsewhere, sculpture is increasingly breaking all the traditional rules, as we have just seen in the examples of Krajcberg, Weissmann, de Camargo, and other sculptors who, having toyed for a while with the figurative, have then passed on to abstract and geometrical forms, in the same way as the painters who took up Abstractism and Concretism. Some painters, too, after Pop art and the rediscovery of objects as pictorial facts, have now begun to invade the territory of sculpture. And they make *boxes*, one of the latest fashions.

In a country where the box, in the form of the small case, more or less decorated and used for keeping holy images, is already a tradition, it is interesting to note that a competitive exhibition of boxes attracted as many as eighty entrants. Some of the artists tried to revive the holy-image case, using it as a recepticle for present-day images, others produced boxes as geometricized sculptures, and there were even those who used electricity for creating optical effects and movement.

Sculpture? Sculpture more than painting, perhaps—or the two arts combined, recalling the application of painting to architecture and sculpture in classical times. But it is all, as in the time of Duchamp, highly entertaining and a great occasion for excited arguments. The same may be said of the *objects* we see nowadays in so many shows. We shall seek in these pages to give due representation to the mental attitudes of the young Brazilian artists who are more than ever anxious to take part in the newest movements, even by launching manifestoes and organizing happenings—which never manage, somehow, to raise a scandal. Conditions at present are not propitious, for it is almost impossible to shift the dust that still lies heavy over the Academies. All this leads to the question of the historical precedents of modern trends in painting, such as Pop art, as we shall see in later pages.

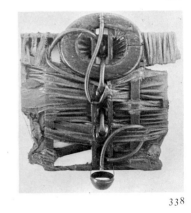

335 A. MORAES. *Box*, 1966. Metals and wood, 40 × 80 cm. Collection of the artist.

336 R. REY. *Power*, 1966. Painted metal and plaster of Paris, height 20 cm. Collection of the artist.

337 L. ZANOTTO. *Totality*, 1965. Relief of paper, masonite, and plastic, 50.5 × 40 cm. Museum of Contemporary Art, São Paulo.

338 D. FERRARI. *Red Object*, 1965. Cloth, iron, wood, and plastic, 97 × 88 cm. Collection of the artist.

339 G. M. HENRIQUE. *Compositions*, 1963. Wood and other materials, 50 × 40 cm. Collection of the artist.

340 E. PUTZOLU. *Connection*, 1966. Wood and plastic threads, 50 × 100 cm. Collection of the artist.

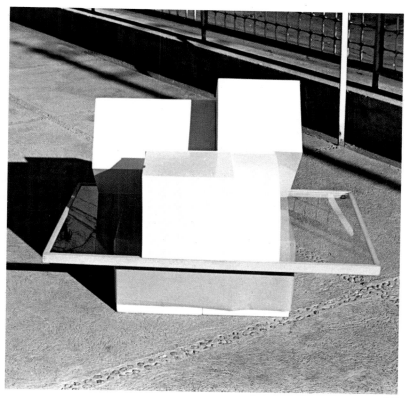

341

342

343

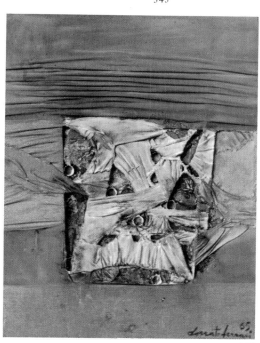

344

345

341 G. M. HENRIQUE. Boxes to be arranged at pleasure, 1967. Painted wood, each box about 30 × 30 × 30 cm. Private collection, São Paulo.

342 H. COUTINHO. *Box*, 1967. Wood and pieces of colored glass, mobile for light effects, 100 × 100 cm. Private collection, São Paulo.

343 D. CAMPOS. *Sexoscope*, 1967. Wood, mirror, and plastic, motorized, 75 × 40 × 40 cm. Collection of the artist.

344 D. FERRARI. *Breakdown Voltage*, 1965. Cloth and vinyl, 180 × 141 cm. Collection of the artist.

345 R. CABOT. *Object*, 1966. Wood, glued and painted, height 33 cm. Collection: Mirante das Artes, São Paulo.

Trends in painting

With the coming of industrialism, especially in the cities of São Paulo and Rio de Janeiro, the question of industrial design suddenly became a matter of importance. In 1950, the Museum of Art at São Paulo, having become aware of the doubt and uncertainty that still reigned in this field, due to a lack of experts and to a lack of demand on the part of the manufacturers (and even of its own publicists, who found it easier to adapt imported projects and designs), added to its various schools one of industrial design, which was a great success with the young. The teachers were architects and artists who had had European experience but were nevertheless convinced that the spirit of the lessons should be Brazilian. Some of the best designers turned out by the school later perfected their studies at the Hochschule für Gestaltung at Ulm under Max Bill, and are now teachers themselves in institutions set up in Brazil for this specialty. Industrial design finds its principal fields of application in the furniture industry and in graphic arts; in the latter, owing to the presence of numerous branches of large international organizations, the Brazilian contribution is only just becoming noticeable.

In the furniture industry, except for some models by Warchavchik inspired by the very Teutonic severity of Gropius's Bauhaus (Segall had some of the originals from Dessau in his home), it was not until about 1947 that local models began to appear, which were also adapted to the Brazilian climate: these were designed by the architect Lina Bo, who taught in the Museum's school of industrial design. Since anything new in Brazil always catches on like wildfire, there was an immediate rush to produce modern, or supposedly modern, furniture, and the very factories that had been happily turning out a hundred or so models of hybrid nineteenth-century styles had finally to bring themselves up to date. This was a welcome vindication of the modernized interior, which in turn helped, and still helps in various ways, the renewal of architecture and the fortunes of the more recent painting. Today Brazil produces well-designed furniture, and models by

the most famous international designers are mass-produced to the highest standards. The availability of some very fine materials, especially woods, traditional craftsmanship, and a sufficient industrial capacity, have made it possible to produce goods that are already appreciated and sold abroad.

In the graphic arts—typographic layout, poster design, advertisement display, catalogue production, etc.—a certain aesthetic independence of the more advanced work in Europe and the United States may be noted. A particularly high standard has been reached in recent years, especially in the production of calendars, where efficient teams of graphic artists and photographers have worked together with imagination and psychological insight.

In photography, too, there are now several good artists. The process was introduced into Brazil in 1840 by the Abbé Combes, and for many years hardly ever departed from its purely documentary purpose of portraiture. But with the arrival of the illustrated magazine it naturally came to be regarded as an art. It was the photo-reporter Jean Manzon who brought new life to photography, and who formed, through his teaching, a group of excellent photographers.

With regard to the design of durable goods, particularly household electric appliances, allowance must be made for the fact that there is now a trend to a standardized functionality that leaves little scope for variation from country to country. Outer casings follow functional lines that are the same for all latitudes, yet many Brazilian examples of industrial design are notable for their formal purity.

There is more freedom from outside influences in the handicraft industries, and this is due to a long heritage of remarkable technical ability and to a fertile and varied popular imagination, assimilated by social circumstances and by having to work in certain materials. Brazil is a synthesis of diverse streams of immigration and the mingling of the most disparate races, yet each people brought their own habits and customs, not to impose them, but to add them to the rest and let them undergo modification. Even the Roman Catholic

Church failed to preserve the integrity of her liturgical symbols: the pineapple displaced the vine, the heron, the dove, and so on, due to a mysterious amalgamating force which was even capable of welcoming the saints of the Church among the benevolent spirits of African religion in a strange and wonderful Elysium.

Popular art is the work of the craftsman; and while it is disappearing in a world full of machinery that does everything, it is a remarkable fact that in Brazil, even if so much is remote and secret, the production of popular art is still a genuine activity. For in this rapidly changing world, in which machines turn out glasses—and, more recently, drinking vessels of waxed carton or plastic—by the million, every market day boats may still be seen leaving the Recôncavo of Bahia laden with household pottery ware, hand made and hand decorated, as if, centuries ago, they were setting out with cargoes of vases from Caere or Knossos.

There is so much luxuriance of form and color in the tropic landscape, and so much variety, that it is impossible to convey a true idea of what it is really like; it is difficult to paint—even to photograph—on account of the continually changing atmosphere, let alone the enormous expanses of territory that break up any panorama and prevent its being reduced to a type. The general vague idea we have of the tropics is much the same as that which the romantic, sentimental nineteenth-century painters gave us of Africa, dominated by the red fire of the sun turning the sky into a rosy, honied sea. Many foreign artists have visited the country, but the real Brazilian landscape has escaped them all. There has been only one painter, perhaps, who might have shown it us in its true light—the great Turner himself. Previously, early in the seventeenth century, the Dutch Painter, Frans Post, who accompanied John Maurice of Nassau, left us some landscapes of Pernambuco: careful topographical delineations with sober colors that give blue tones to hills and fields, and with perfect definition of light. After Post, landscape painting was abandoned, and when attempts

346 Exhibition at São Paulo, 1967.   Photo by José Xavier.

were made to revive it they lapsed into conventionality.

But the natural landscape itself, stupendous and mysterious, which four centuries ago took de Léry's breath away, is still there to offer inspiration, to suggest new points of departure or approach. With its striking variety, its vast wilderness of tangled forest, its tortuous rivers with their spectacular falls, its immense desert regions, its oceans breaking endlessly on its coasts, its skies that disgorge torrential rains, it is not easy to arrive at a comprehensive view; it must be built up piecemeal by logical process. From this earthly paradise not even the Indian tribes themselves have taken more than a few hints, such as the phallic form symbolic of procreation, which is common to all primitive peoples, a certain degree of anthropomorphic design in the decoration of sun-baked terracottas, simple featherwork, and childish geometrical motifs. The first colonists, who brought an already fully-developed art from the Iberian peninsula were induced by the new surroundings to remodel their forms, and even at times to invent new ones, and to make an almost idolatrous

use of the color of gold, deadening the more vivacious colors with over-use of ochers. Only the Negroes have been able to enliven the general grayness of artistic initiative with tones of fantasy, brilliance of hue, and that special flavor to be discerned in form, color, rhythm, and dance, all of which are still today characteristic features of Brazilian vitality, whose most famous manifestation is the yearly carnival.

Has all this choreographic and figurative splendor (one need only think of the samba schools, of the spiritual rites of Roman Catholicism, of the tense liveliness of popular music) had any influence on contemporary art? It is difficult to say. Some European artists who have settled in Brazil have taken superficial note of this rich natural and human material, but they have not troubled to go into it deeply, to absorb it, or to discover any inner spiritual meanings; they have rarely stirred beyond the Europeanized cities, continuing their lives with their bodies on the Tropic of Capricorn and their minds beyond the ocean. Only in the northeast, owing to the different environmental conditions, have a few native artists been able to

penetrate the meaning of the system and its outward expression, and to understand its symbols. Among them, in the first rank, are Cícero Dias and Lula Cardoso Ayres, who, in the region where tradition is most respected (or possibly the only region where it is respected at all), have surpassed all others in identifying themselves with the spirit of the people that are the creators of the most ebullient folk-lore in America.

To find anything like it in the south one is forced to search among the untutored Sunday painters, who are the unconscious recorders and relators of the real nature of the land and the genuine humor of the people. This is the reason for the inclusion of some of these painters in the following pages— after the figurative painters of, let us say, a certain professional eminence, who have chosen subjects from the same emotional atmosphere.

Fios de telegrafo
Muros corroidos pela chuva com tijolos vermelhos à vista
Flores artificiais
Papel de sedã
Peninha de pombo suspensa no ar
Borboletas
Moscas azuis tipicas da periferia
Cafeteira sem fundo
Libélulas
Bacias furadas
Despertadores a tilintar
Aneis de noivado
Filó branco

vaca típica da periferia

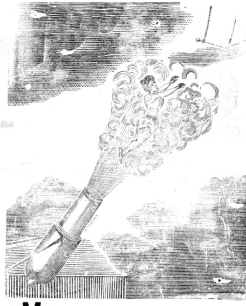

Vem **Vem**

ao Baile **O ARRABALDE**

347

348

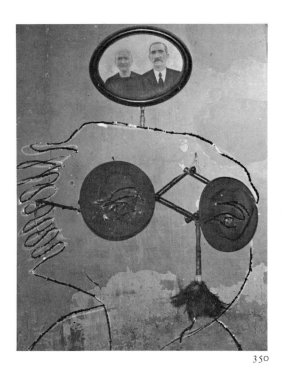

In the next few pages we shall see something of the work of the 'visual operators', artists who devote themselves to techniques of 'comunication', a term that may cover anything from an ideogram so arcane that only initiates who know the secret wavelength can get the message to the spelling-book clarity of a character in a comic-strip. The transmitter of these messages is usually New York, which is nothing to take exception to for either the intent or the effect; but they encircle the globe and are received in Brazil, whereupon they are refashioned by people who are crazy about anything new and then relayed, particularly to the provinces, where they are sometimes mistaken for genuine and original ideas. And this is only one contributory element in the madly chaotic atmosphere in which we live and which we must learn to put up with just as we put up with the wind and the rain.

349

350

351 Happening at the Rex Gallery, São Paulo, 1967.

352 Exhibition of aircraft components presented as art objects, Bahia State Museum of Modern Art, Salvador, 1960.

We may begin with some of the more up-to-date trends. So-called Pop art, however, is by no means a novelty to certain artists in Brazil, as may be seen from these examples which predate the recent doctrine that junk can be good art material.

347 Décor for a ball organized by L. Bo at the Clube dos Artistas e Amigos da Arte at São Paulo, 1950. The ball was entitled 'Outskirts', and the décor consisted of all the staple commodities of the rubbish dump: empty cans, twisted metal, rusty tins, scrap-metal, broken dolls, broken bottles, rags, dilapidated objects, rotten rope, and rusty wire—a veritable example of trashbin aesthetics.

348 Invitation to the ball made up of old last-century typographical material and in a style of lay-out that a few years later would have been called Pop. The ball was something of a scandal: the artists came, but the more rewarding public in box-office terms, the café society that generally goes to such entertainments, was scared off by the rubbish and the invitation, which were taken as an insult.

349 G. DE BARROS. *Face*, 1950. Tempera and old shoe, 70 × 50 cm. Original destroyed.

350 G. DE BARROS. *Parents*, 1950. Montage of photograph, phial, hats, hat-rack, feather duster, and wire, 100 × 100 cm. Original destroyed.

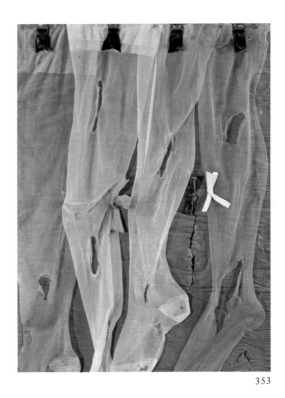

353

354

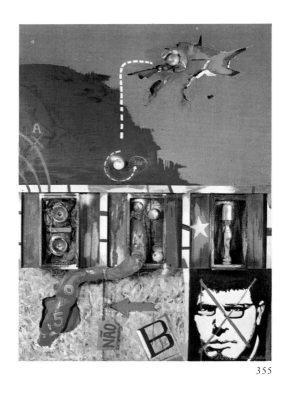

355

356

357

353 M. GOROVITZ. *O toi, que j'eusse*, 1965. Textile fabrics and metal, 69 × 50 cm. Collection of the artist.
354 L. NEVES TAVARES DE ALMEIDA. *The Meaning of Evolution*, 1966. Clockwork composition on iron tondo, diam. 50 cm. Collection of the artist.
355 K. TOMOSHIGUE. Untitled, 1965. Oil and objects on board, 169 × 120 cm. Collection of the artist.
356 B. VACCARINI. *Composition 304*, 1964. Tinplate and iron, height 100 cm. Collection of the artist.
357 W. CORDEIRO. *Bitter*, 1965. Lettering on taut cloth with flashing light behind, 50 × 70 × 10 cm. Collection of the artist.

358

359

360

358–360 W. D. LEE. *The Trapezium, or A Confession*, 1965. Suspended chamber consisting of four walls, two of which painted in oils on both sides, two of acrylic, and heliciform canopy with electronic sound apparatus, 200 × 200 × 200 cm. Collection of the artist.

361 W. D. LEE. *The Zone, or Four Graces*, 1966. Oil on canvasses against background. Collection of the artist.

page 90

362 M. SCHENDEL. *The Return of Achilles*, 1965. Oil on canvas, 92 × 130 cm. Collection of the artist.

363 J. R. AGUILAR. *Myth II*, 1966. Spray on canvas, 114 × 146 cm. Collection of the artist.

364 V. PASQUALINI. *The Cause*, 1964–5. Oil on paper with relief in wood, cotton, and nylon, 110 × 80 cm. Collection of the artist.

365 M. CHIAVERINI. *Drawing*, 1965. Litho pencil and impression on flong, 100 × 70 cm. Collection: Giacomo del Valle. São Paulo.

366 M. NOGUEIRA LIMA. *Help! Helpening*, 1965. Oil on board, 80 × 80 cm. Collection of the artist.

367 M. CARAM. *Bestiality*, 1964. Ink drawing, 100 × 70 cm. Collection of the artist.

368 R. BARRIENTOS. *Drawing 2*, 1965. Gouache on canvas, 130 × 80 cm. Collection of the artist.

369 U. MOTTA LIMA. *An Adjective Expresses the Quality of a Thing*, 1965. Oil on board and collage, 35 × 70 cm. Collection of the artist.

370 J. A. VAN ACKER. *The Landing of Publicity*, 1961. Oil on board, triptych 160 × 220 cm. Museum of Contemporary Art, São Paulo.

371 L. BARAVELLI. *Haydn Concerto*, 1967. Oil on canvas, 73 × 100 cm. Collection of the artist.

361

362

363

364

365

366

368

367

369

370

371

372

373

374

372 A. DIAS. *Letter*, 1965. Indian ink and gouache, 40 × 30 cm. Collection of the artist.
373 C. A. VERGARA. *Figure*, 1965. Oil on canvas, 100 × 81 cm. Private collection, São Paulo.
374 A. DIAS. *Emblem*, 1967. Gouache on canvas, 30 × 40 cm. Collection: Galerie Delta, Rotterdam.
375 R. GERCHMAN. *Football*, 1965. Industrial paint on duratex, 100 × 70 cm. Collection of the artist.

375

376

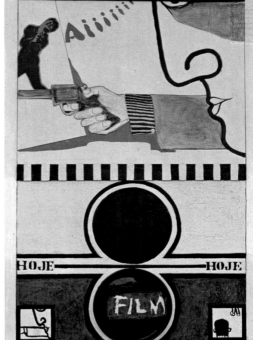

377

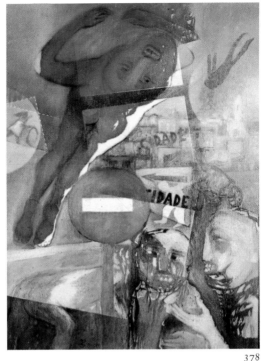

378

379

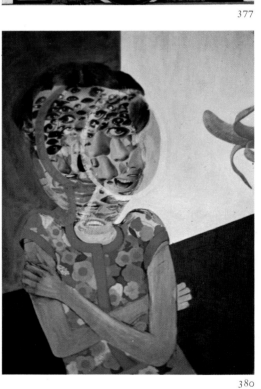

380

381

382

376 S. FERRO. *Composition*, 1965. Gouache on plaster of Paris and masonite, 80 × 70 cm. Regional Museum, Campina Grande, Paraíba.

377 S. SZPIGEL. *Cinema*, 1966. Mixed media on board, 100 × 80 cm. Collection of the artist.

378 B. SILVA. *Blue City Ghost*, 1966. Oil on canvas, 120 × 90 cm. Collection of the artist.

379 F. IMPERIO. *March*, 1965. Oil, metals, and relief on board, 40 × 40 cm. Collection of the artist.

380 J. RÊA. *She and her Banana*, 1965. Oil and collage on canvas. 100 × 80 cm. Collection of the artist.

381 T. NAZAR. *Memory of my Grandmother*, 1967. Oil, metals, plexiglas, and plaster of Paris on board, 110 × 80 cm. Collection of the artist.

382 F. J. NASSER. *Drawing*, 1967. Gouache and indian ink on paper, 64 × 48 cm. Collection of the artist.

383

384

383 and 384 N. LEIRNER. *Adoration*, 1966. Oleographs, painting, neon tube, 205 × 165 cm., in a circular curtained sanctum, diam. 270 cm., beyond a turnstile. The central painting portrays the pop singer Roberto Carlos, idol of teenagers. Museum of Art, São Paulo.
385 J. RESENDE. *Nuptials on the Magic Carpet*, 1967. Aluminium, velvet, tulle, and plastic, 200 × 70 × 60 cm. Collection of the artist.

385

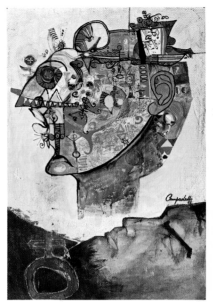

386

387

388

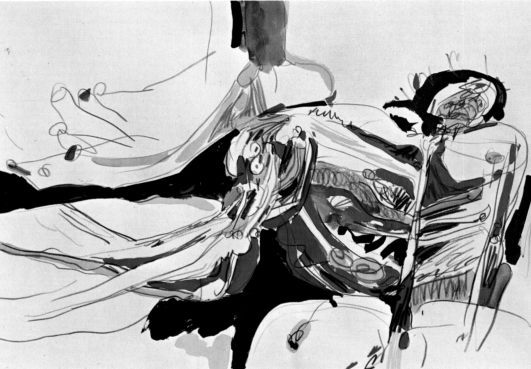

389

390

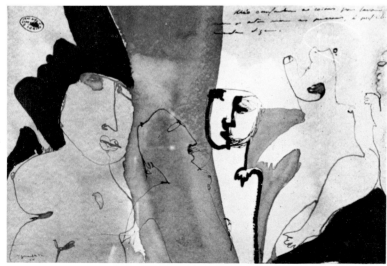

391

386 V. I. MONTEIRO. *Thousands of Medals*, 1965. Oil on canvas, 120 × 100 cm. Museum of Art, Belo Horizonte.

387 I. SERPA. *The Repentant*, 1965. Gouache on paper, 60 × 45 cm. Collection of the Artist.

388 R. CAMPADELLO. *Mask and Neurosis*, 1965. Oil on canvas, 100 × 65 cm. Museum of Art, São Paulo.

389 F. MAGALHÃES. *Figures*, 1965. Gouache and indian ink on paper, 100 × 70 cm. Collection of the artist.

390 H. SAPIA. *Allusions*, 1966. Gouache and crayon on paper, 50 × 70 cm. Collection: Mirante das Artes, São Paulo.

391 R. VATER. *Watercolor*, 1966. Gouache on paper, 35 × 45 cm. Collection: Mirante das Artes, São Paulo.

392

393

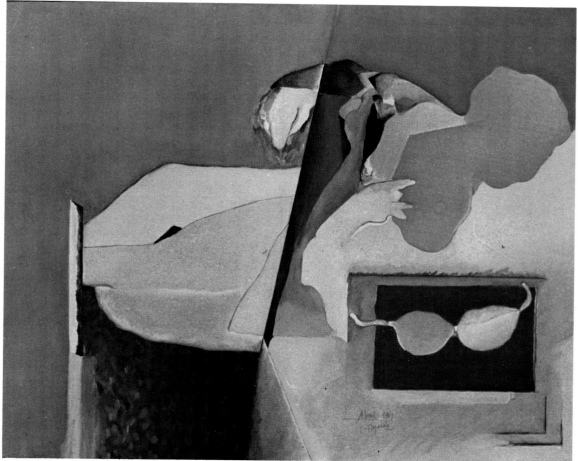

392 and 393 M. H. CHARTUNI. *Diptych of Elizabeth Taylor*, 1967. Oil on board, acrylic, and aluminium, 123 × 100 cm. Private collection, São Paulo.

394 C. A. FAJARDO. *Painting*, 1967. Oil on canvas, 90 × 110 cm. Collection of the artist.

394

395

396

397

395 O. MESTRINER. *Little Cars Repeated,* 1964. Ink drawing and collage on card, 69 × 44 cm. Collection of the artist.

396 TIAGO. *Forest,* 1965. Oil on canvas, 62 × 100 cm. Collection of the artist.

397 B. KING. *Dove over the City,* 1965. Gouache on paper, 40 × 55 cm. Collection of the artist.

398 M. L. LEÃO. *Landscape,* 1964. Oil on canvas, 49 × 90 cm. Private collection, Rio de Janeiro.

399 A. BRILL. *Dwellings,* 1965. Gouache on paper, 50 × 34 cm. Collection of the artist.

400 C. CRUZ. *City,* 1964. Oil on canvas, 100 × 100 cm. Collection: Tavares, Rio de Janeiro.

401 J. MORI. *Île de la Cité,* 1962. Oil on board, 50 × 65 cm. Collection: V. Day, Paris.

402 T. BONAZZOLA. *Landscape at Ouro Prêto,* 1956. Oil on canvas, 50 × 66 cm. Collection: Pola Rezende, São Paulo.

403 M. C. MANUEL GISMONDI. *The Night is Always Green,* 1954. Oil on canvas, 46 × 55 cm. Collection: Galeria Seta, São Paulo.

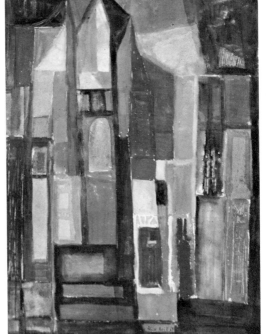

399

400

398

401

402

403

404

405

In a note on Poletti in the Italian art review, *Paragone*, edited by Roberto Longhi, Giovanni Testori wrote as follows: 'At a time when painters are subjecting expression to posture here at last is one who subjects—and with what force!—posture to expression. Here, indeed, there is coincidence, but in the old and still valid sense in that it constitutes the expression of art. In the sense, that is, that posture coincides with the necessity to express a particular existential attitude. It is precisely in this return to informal coincidence that Poletti effects the revision of the facts of modern painting that stand at the back of him. Not that he lets himself be tempted to perform exercises on these facts. Nothing could be further from a personality such as his—so ardent, so perpetually on the alert, like a hunter advancing through a wood, ever on the qui vive for the ever imminent and ever possible appearance of the quarry. In this case, the wood is the urban jungle, and the quarry the deformities, the injustice, and the injuries that civilization—or modern civilization—inflicts on the mind and body of man.'

404 R. POLETTI. *Boxer*, 1965. Oil on canvas, 180 × 160 cm. Private collection, Milan.

405 R. POLETTI. *Stadium*, 1965. Oil on canvas, 180 × 160 cm. Private collection, São Paulo.

406 A. BARBOSO. *Landslide*, 1965. Oil on canvas, 118 × 95 cm. Collection: N. Krautmann, São Paulo.

406

A large number of foreign painters have settled in Brazil, many of them coming from Europe before World War II, and their contribution has been of considerable weight. A few examples are given on this page, headed by J. Golyscheff, who, having lost all his work under the Nazi regime, took refuge in hospitable Brazil.

407 J. GOLYSCHEFF. *Drawing*, from *Der Cicerone*, 1919. Original lost.

408 J. GOLYSCHEFF. *Victory*, 1964. Oil on canvas, 116 × 81 cm. Museum of Contemporary Art, São Paulo.

409 F. DOMINGOS. *Drawing*, 1953. Collection of the artist.

410 H. BOESE. *Composition*, 1960. 100 × 60 cm. Collection of the artist.

411 S. FLEXOR. *The Biped*, 1967. Oil on canvas, 190 × 135 cm. Collection of the artist.

407

408

409

410

411

412

413

412 B. CID DE SOUZA. *Hiroshima No. 2*, 1965. Gouache on canvas, 150 × 113 cm. Collection of the artist.
413 B. CID DE SOUZA. *Look*, 1967. Gouache on canvas, 147 × 114 cm. Collection of the artist.
414 E. JARDIM. *Etching*, 1966. 25.5 × 29.5 cm. Private collection, São Paulo.

414

415   416   417

418   419

420

415 J. M. DE SOUZA. *Waiting*, 1965. Oil on canvas, 66 × 48 cm. Collection: Buck, São Paulo.
416 R. SILVEIRA. *Flight*, 1966. Oil on canvas, 60 × 100 cm. Collection of the artist.
417 W. VIRGOLINO. *Figures*, 1963. Oil on board, 78 × 64 cm. Private collection, São Paulo.
418 A. PEDROSO D'HORTA. *Portrait of the Artist's Mother*, 1950. Oil on canvas, 65 × 50 cm. Museum of Art, São Paulo.
419 L. A. KEATING. *Drawing*, 1966. Ink on paper, 30 × 48 cm. Private collection, São Paulo.
420 Z. BETTIOL. *Ring a Ring o' Roses*, 1966. Wood-engraving, 31 × 46 cm. Museum of Art, São Paulo.

421

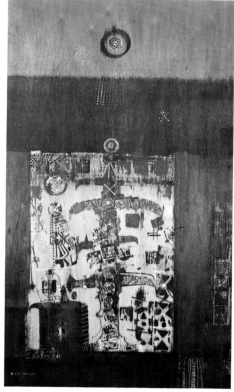

423

422

424

425

421 J. RIBEIRO. *Drawing*, 1963. Ink on paper, 36 × 51 cm. Private collection, São Paulo.

422 F. ODRIOZOLA. *Composition*, 1965. Indian inks and oil on board, 80 × 50 cm. Collection: Miguel Forte, São Paulo.

423 D. VALENÇA LINS. *Landscape with Horsemen*, 1965. Oil on canvas, 60 × 92 cm. Private collection, São Paulo.

424 I. PONS. *Horizon*, 1965. Relief etching, 60 × 40 cm. Collection of the artist.

425 D. VALENÇA LINS. *Topography*, 1965. Water-color, indian ink, and walnut stain, 50 × 60 cm. Collection of the artist.

426 J. FREITAS. *Landscape of Tomorrow*, 1965. Oil and collage on board, 60 × 80 cm. Collection of the artist.

427 A. ZALUAR. *Forest*, 1964. Indian ink on paper, 100 × 70 cm. Collection of the artist.

426

427

428

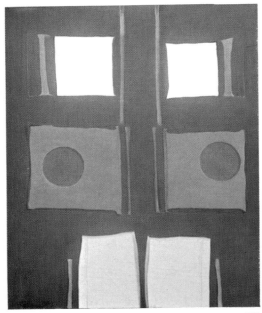
429

430

428 M. L. DA COSTA. *Episode*, 1959. Oil on canvas,
81 × 116 cm. Collection of the artist.
429 M. L. DA COSTA. *Banner*, 1965. Oil on canvas,
110 × 80 cm. Collection: Roberto de Azevedo, São
Paulo.
430 M. DA COSTA. *Figure*, 1948. Oil on canvas,
55 × 47 cm. Collection: Gilberto Chateaubriand, Rio.

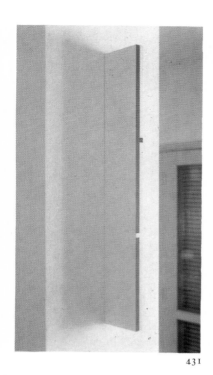 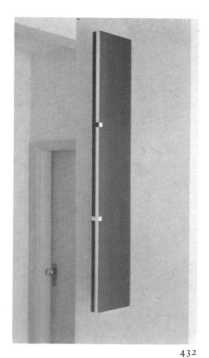 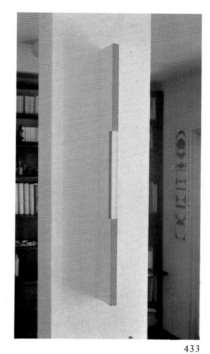 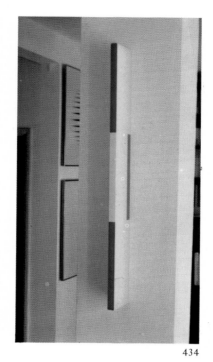

431   432   433   434

The movement of Concrete art in Brazil, it may be noted, really originated with an exhibition of the work of the Swiss designer, Max Bill, organized by the Museum of Art, São Paulo, in 1952. The exhibition, which was very carefully prepared and represented every aspect of the artist's work, was ignored by the press, but a few artists profited from its lesson.

431 and 432 WILLYS DE CASTRO. *Active Object*, April 1961. Oil on canvas on wood, 68.8 × 11.3 × 2.2 cm. Collection of the artist.

433 and 434 WILLYS DE CASTRO. *Active Object*, January 1961. Oil on canvas on wood, 92 × 11.5 × 2.4 cm. Private collection, São Paulo.

435 Exhibition of works by H. BARSOTTI, São Paulo, 1967.

435

436

437

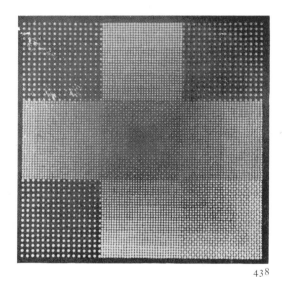

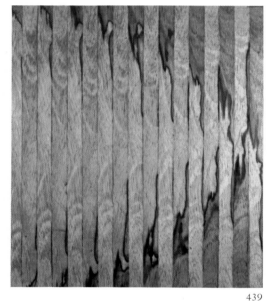

438

439

440

441

442

436 G. RODRIGUES. *Paintings to be Seen through Glasses*, 1967.

437 F. DE LEMOS. Untitled, 1965. Oil on canvas, 90 × 90 cm. Collection: Jorge Fernandes de Carvalho.

438 A. MAVIGNIER. *Crossing*, 1961. Drawing. Collection of the artist.

439 A. PALATNIK. *Progression 96-A*, 1965. Composition in wood, 57 × 48 cm. Collection of the artist.

440 F. DE LEMOS. *Design, Ser. 2, No. 9*, 1958. Ink on paper, 70 × 45 cm. Private collection, São Paulo.

441 A. PALATNIK. Images produced by a projection instrument. Brazil has not lacked disciples of the French Jesuit, Louis-Bertrand Cartel, the inventor of the 'clavecin oculaire', mentioned in Rousseau's *Confessions*. Since the days of the kaleidoscope modern technology has evolved far more elaborate 'lumino-dynamic' instruments, and of the various practitioners of this art form in Brazil Palatnik is the most interesting.

442 V. MACIEL. *Painting*, 1967. Acrylic on canvas, 120 × 80 cm. Collection of the artist.

443

444

443 A. DE CASTRO. *Sculpture*, 1961. Welded sheet-iron, 130 × 50 × 15 cm. Collection of the artist.

444 Exhibition of Neo-Concretism, São Paulo, 1961. In the background, suspended *Non-Objects* by H. OITICICA; in the middle distance, *Bichos* by L. CLARK; in the foreground, two *Non-Object Poems* by FERREIRA GULLAR.

445 and 448 FERREIRA GULLAR. *Remembrance* (Non-Object Poem), 1959. Wood, 40 × 40 cm. Removal of the blue cube reveals the legend LEMBRA (remembrance). The experiment arose from the search for a non-syntactical language.

446 L. CLARK. *Sundial*, 1960. Aluminium. Private collection, Rio. The novelty in these objects by Lygia Clark is that the spectator is invited to participate actively in the rearrangement of her 'bichos'—i.e. 'beasts' or self-moving creatures—by exploiting their representational possibilities as he likes.

447 L. CLARK. *Vestiary sculpture*, 1967. This represents the artist's latest phase.

445

446

448

447

449

450

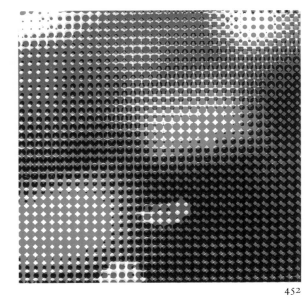

451

452

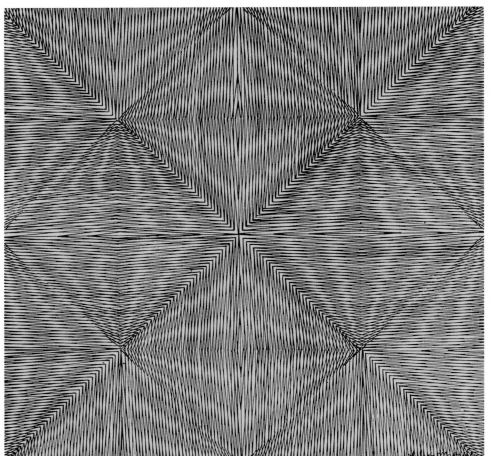

453

454

455

456

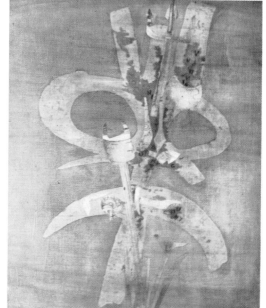

459

457

458

The visual operators, or visual researchers, already form a considerable group. They take note of what is being done elsewhere and experiment unpretentiously with new materials and new ideas, and with various combinations between these and the traditional techniques, and so produce effects which reveal hitherto unsuspected means of communication.

449 A. ALIBERTI. Untitled, 1966. Modulated stainless steel, 45 × 100 cm. Collection of the artist.

450 L. CHAROUX. Drawing, 1966. Gouache and casein on paper. Collection of the artist.

451 H. KÜHN. Reflection Problem, 1966. Acrylic on styropor, 100 × 100 cm. Collection of the artist.

452 H. FIAMINGHI. Color-Light Screen, 1961–6. Litho-offset of fusion and diffusion of color from incidence of light, 70 × 70 cm. Collection of the artist.

453 S. M. GUELLER. Drawing No. 3, 1966. Ink and gouache on card, 52 × 52 cm. Collection of the artist.

454 F. KAZMER. Impact, 1966. Acrylic and polyester, 42 × 39 cm. Collection of the artist.

455 R. VALENTIM. Group of works photographed in the artist's studio in Rome, 1965.

456 E. RAMOSA. Composition, 1964. Oil on canvas, 100 × 66 cm. Collection of the artist.

457 A. ROSSI. Instruments of Macumba, 1967. Oil and collage on canvas, 50 × 40 cm. Collection of the artist.

458 S. BAENDERECK. Sign-writing, 1966. Oil on canvas, 100 × 70 cm. Collection of the artist.

459 A. TEIXEIRA. Composition, 1965. Oil on canvas, 140 × 100 cm. Collection of the artist.

Surrealism did not thrive in Brazil; it was not, that is to say, introduced from abroad, in spite of two notorious visits by Benjamin Péret in about 1930 and 1957, both of which ended in his expulsion for political reasons.

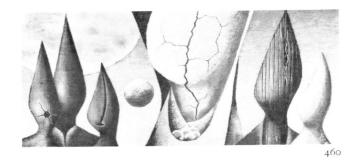

460

461

462

463

464

465

466

460 W. LEVY. *Painting*, 1965. Oil on canvas, 55 × 120 cm. Collection of the artist.

461 Z. ANDRADE LIMA. *Faces and Phantoms*, 1966. Ink drawing, 50 × 70 cm. Collection of the artist.

462 TRINIDADE LEAL. *Wild Cat Pursuing Armadillos*, 1964. Woodcut, 25 × 37 cm.

463 WAGNER DE CASTRO. *Liberation*, 1965. Oil on canvas, 98 × 46 cm. Collection of the artist.

464 E. BUENO. *Preceding Life*, 1962. Ink drawing, 52 × 38 cm. Collection of the artist.

465 CELSO. *Drawing*, 1966. Indian ink, 70 × 25 cm. Collection of the artist.

466 M. V. POETZCHER. *Drawing*, 1965. Indian ink, 65 × 47 cm. Collection of the artist.

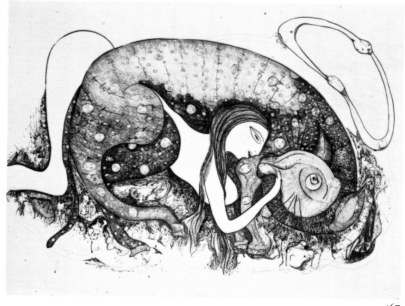

467

468

469

470

471

472

467 M. C. BASTOS. *Lady and Jaguar*, 1965. Ink drawing on paper, 50 × 75 cm. Collection: Fábio Ribeiro, Rio.
468 M. GRASSMANN. *Battle*, 1964. Sepia drawing on paper, 50 × 66 cm. Private collection, São Paulo.
469 E. HIRSCH. *The Lass Menagerie: a Bountiful Bestiary of Fauna-guised Females*, from *Playboy*, December 1965.
470 N. XANDÓ. *Painting 1*, 1965. Oil on canvas, 116 × 81 cm. Collection of the artist.
471 A. A. BRANDÃO. *Witch*, 1965. Ink drawing on cloth, 66 × 95 cm. Collection of the artist.
472 I. BATISTESA SAPIA. *Apparitions*, 1966. Oil on canvas, 70 × 100 cm. Collection of the artist.

473

474

475

476

473 J. CÂMARA F. *Painting*, 1965. Encaustic and oil on wood, 220 × 160 cm. Collection of the artist.

474 P. RISSONE. *Disenchanted Child*, 1962. Gouache on paper, 70 × 50 cm. Collection: F. Milan.

475 A. H. AMARAL. *Dialogue*, 1966. Woodcut, 54 × 80 cm. Collection: Mirante das Artes, São Paulo.

476 T. SANTA ROSA. *Face*, 1956. Pencil drawing, 36 × 32 cm. Whereabouts unknown.

477

478

482

479

480

481

484

483

477 L. ABRAMO. Woodcut, 1951. 40 × 20 cm. Collection of the artist. In about 1960 Abramo started an Atelier de Gravure at São Paulo, which had considerable success and did much to spread the taste for the woodcut.

478 R. MAGALHÃES. *Arrival of the Enemy*, 1965. Woodcut, 32 × 48 cm. Collection of the artist.

479 W. G. NASSIF. *Electra and her Brother*, 1964. Woodcut, 30 × 30 cm. Museum of Contemporary Art, São Paulo.

480 HANSEN-BAHIA. Illustration from *Begegnung mit Hansen-Bahia* by Jürgen Beckelmann, Darmstadt, 1960.

481 CALAZANS NETO. *Street in Bahia*, 1964. Woodcut, 14 × 8 cm. Collection of the artist.

482 N. CAVALCANTI. *Miraculous Fruit*, 1965. Woodcut, 30 × 30 cm. Collection of the artist.

483 P. LAZZAROTTO. *Cowhouse*, 1950. Etching.

484 M. D. BARTHOLO. *Woodcut*, 1965. 36 × 50 cm. Collection of the artist.

485

486

487

488

489

490

491

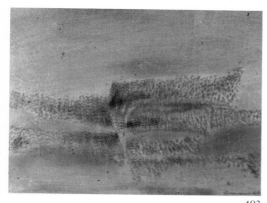

492

493

494

495

496

497

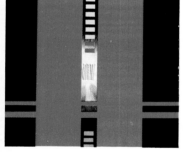

499

500

498

501

502

Folk-lore and popular legend, especially in the cities of Recife and Salvador, offer rich and interesting subjects for art, and sometimes receive perceptive interpretation, but often merely serve as illustrative material for tourist publicity.

485 L. CARDOSO AYRES. *Figures of the 'Bumba-meu-boi'*, 1945. Oil on canvas, 78 × 100 cm. Collection of the artist.

486 G. SAMICO. *Leaf-Eater*, 1962. Woodcut, 44 × 40 cm. Collection of the artist.

487 CARYBÉ. *The Armed Band*, 1965. Oil on canvas, 74 × 100 cm. Collection: R. Saboia Pessoa, Salvador.

488 Photograph of a *Cangaçeiro*, state of Bahia, about 1940.

489 A. MARTINS. *Figure*, 1967. Drawing, 100 × 100 cm. Regional Museum, Campina Grande, Paraiba.

490 Actors of the Brazilian Folk-lore Theater, 1961. Director, M. ASKANASY.

491 M. PERETTI. *Maractú*, 1963. Oil on canvas, 33 × 41 cm. Museum of Art, Olinda, Recife.
Abstractism has had a tremendous vogue in Brazil and attracted numerous bands of amateurs who have invaded the exhibitions. Most of the figurative painters adapted their manner to the new style, only to abandon it when new fashions came in. It is not an easy matter to give a comprehensive selection of the so-called informal painting, but some works of the artists most representative of the movement are shown on this page.

492 S. ESMERALDO. *Landscape*, 1966. Gouache on paper, 39 × 53 cm. Collection: Mirante das Artes, São Paulo.

493 L. PÉRSIO. *Composition*, 1965. Oil on canvas, 50 × 50 cm. Collection of the artist.

494 V. BARCELOS. *Forms in Movement*, 1965. Woodcut, 25 × 37 cm. Collection of the artist.

495 M. POLO. *Composition*, 1965. Oil on canvas, 114 × 146 cm. Collection: Professor Flexa Ribeiro, Rio.

496 Y. MOHALY. *A Red Disk*, 1964. Oil on canvas, 150 × 130 cm. Society of Modern Art, London.

497 F. OSTROWER. *Composition*, 1965. Woodcut, 30 × 70 cm. Collection of the artist.

498 A. JANELLI. *Composition*, 1965. Gouache, 100 × 70 cm. Collection of the artist.

499 A. B. GEIGER. *Family*, 1965. Aquatint, relief, and etching, 24.5 × 49.5 cm.

500 A. DE SOUZA. *Composition*, 1966. Printing inks on paper, 35 × 57 cm. Collection of the artist.

501 J. ANDRADE CAVALCANTI. *Composition*, 1967. Collage, 18 × 20 cm. Collection of the artist.

502 W. NERI. *Melancholy*, 1966. Oil on canvas, 60 × 120 cm. Collection: Miss Aquino, New York.

503

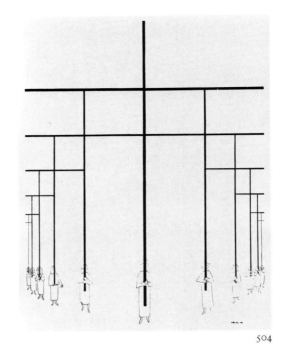

504

505

506

507

508

509

510

511

512

513

514

515

516

517

518

Devotees of the spirit of irony are not numerous; Brazilians are ready enough to laugh at themselves, but they are more likely to do so in literary epigrams than in the arts of design. One who has achieved some fame, however, is Millôr Fernandes, an appealing and melancholy observer of the absurdity of life.

503 M. FERNANDES. Illustration from *O Cruzeiro*, 1961.

504 M. FERNANDES. *At Mondrian's Funeral*, 1957. Pen-and-ink drawing.

505 PERICLES. Illustration from *O Cruzeiro*, 1943. This sketch, in the Rio weekly *O Cruzeiro*, marked the first appearance of the Friend of the Jaguar, a characteristic and popular feature still appearing regularly.

506 M. FERNANDES. Illustration from *Pif-Paf*, 1963.

507 FORTUNA. Illustration from the daily *Correio da Manhã*, 1966.

508 H. WEBER. Illustration from the daily *O Estado de São Paulo*, 1966.

509 C. ESTEVÃO. Illustration from *O Cruzeiro*, 1966.

510 OTAVIO. Illustration from the daily *Ultima Hora*, 1966.

511 JAGUAR. Illustration from *O Senhor*, 1960.

512 ZIRALDO. Illustration from the daily *Correio da Manhã*, 1966.

The great majority of artists are competent professionals who turn out work in the more conventional modes on themes acceptable to the middle classes such as landscapes, figures, still lives, and religious subjects. Together with the folk-lore specialists they enjoy a popularity that is assured to them by the press, and this results in what might be called Decoration—an art, that is to say, with no inherent problems and making no pretence of appealing to the taste of a society that is, in fact, still in process of formation and not yet much preoccupied with social questions. Of this numerous group of professional artists we offer a selection of some of the most highly considered names.

513 E. MARCIER. *Rua do Ouvidor*, 1964. Oil on canvas, 50 × 60 cm. Collection: Gilberto Chateaubriand, Rio.

514 A. GUTIERREZ. *Two Wardrobes with Mirrors*, 1966. Tempera on hardboard, 92 × 52.5 cm. Private collection, Rio.

515 C. SCLIAR. *Coffee-pot and Flowers*, 1965. Collage and vinyl, 56.5 × 37.5 cm. Collection: Galeria Gemini, Rio.

516 M. GRUBER. *Moonlight of Stone*, 1966. Oil on canvas, 100 × 70 cm. Collection of the artist.

517 D. PENTEADO. *Christ*, 1966. Oil and collage on canvas, 150 × 150 cm. Private collection.

518 C. BASTOS. *Balloons*, 1961. Oil on canvas, 92 × 73 cm. Regional Museum, Campina Grande, Paraiba.

519

520

521

522

523

524

We may conclude our review of the figurative artists with a glance at some of the most figurative of them all—the illustrators in black and white and the designers of comics and strips. There was a time when Brazil imported comics; today she is on the way to exporting them. A book by J. Cortez, *A Técnica do desegno*, published in 1966, gives examples of the work of as many as twenty-six black-and-white artists, some of which are shown on this page.

519 A. THOMAS. *Utter Confusion.*
520 L. SAYDENBERG. *'Come here... Ow!!!'*
521 J. W. RODRIGUES. *The Execution of Tiradentes.*
522 M. VICTOR F. *Indian Attacking a Bandeirante.*
523 M. DE SOUZA. *Drawing.*
524 L. ARAGÃO. *Strip.*
525 J. CORTEZ. *Drawing.*
526 O. PIZZI. *Saci Pereré.*
527 M. DE MELLO. *Strip.*
528 J. LANZELLOTI. *The Cangaçeiro.*

525

526

527

528

530

529

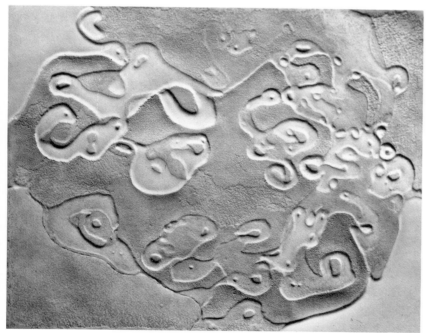

531

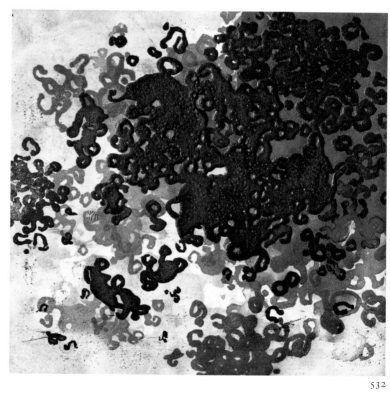

532

529 R. DELAMONICA. *No. 53*, 1965. Etching, 34 × 34 cm. Collection of the artist.

530 R. DELAMONICA. *Composition*, 1965. Etching, 29 × 29 cm. Collection: M. Berckwitz, Rio.

531 ROSSINI PEREZ. *Decoration*, 1965. Engraving, etching, and relief in metal, 25 × 31 cm. Forsythe Gallery, Michigan, U.S.A.

532 ROSSINI PEREZ. *Agitation*, 1964. Engraving, etching, and relief in metal, 35 × 35 cm. Collection: Philippe Guy Woog, Geneva.

533

534

535

536

537

538

539

533 A. BANDEIRA. *Sunlight on a Landscape*, 1966. Oil on canvas, 130 × 97 cm. Collection of the artist.

534 A. BANDEIRA. *Nucleus in Expansion*, 1965. Oil on canvas, 212 × 150 cm. Collection of the artist.

535 I. CAMARGO. *Panel*, 1967. Oil on canvas, 700 × 700 cm. World Health Organization Building, Geneva.

536 and 537 Exhibition of paintings by A. Bandeira at the Bahia State Museum of Modern Art, Salvador, 1960.

538 A. PIZA. *The Red Sun*, 1965. Gouge-engraving on copper, 48 × 36 cm. Collection: Éditions La Hune, Paris.

539 A. PIZA. *Mosaic*, 1965. Paper and sand on wooden base, 37 × 29 cm. Collection of the artist.

541

540

542

543

544

545

546

547

540 S. BRANNIGAN. *Painting*, 1965. Oil on canvas, 150 × 120 cm. Collection of the artist.

541 D. LAZZARINI. *Crowded Wharf*, 1966. Mixed media, 63 × 100 cm. Collection: Edmundo Marco, Rio.

542 F. SCHAEFFER. *Machine*, 1965. Gouache, 70 × 100 cm. Collection of the artist.

543 G. RODRIGUES. *Painting R-50*, 1964. Vinyl on canvas, 184 × 240 cm. Collection of the artist.

544 N. GUERRA. *Composition*, 1964. Oil on canvas, 75 × 65 cm. Collection: Wesley Duke Lee.

545 E. SMYTHE. *Painting No. 165*, 1965. Oil on canvas, 65 × 81 cm. Collection of the artist.

546 H. WONG. *Summer*, 1965. Oil on canvas, 80 × 100 cm. Collection of the artist.

547 C. PILÓ. *Composition*, 1965. Water-color, 53 × 24 cm. Museum of Art, São Paulo.

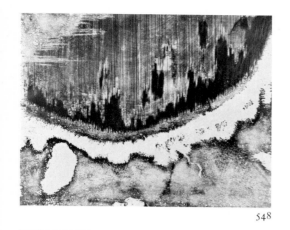

548

549

550

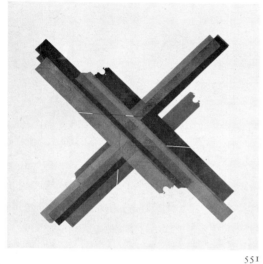

551

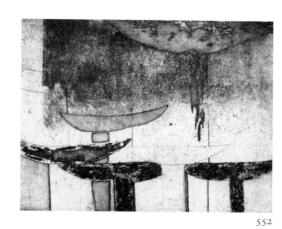

552

553

554

555

556

557

548 D. BASTOS. *Wood-engraving*, 1963. 32 × 43 cm. Collection of the artist.

549 A. LETICIA. *Etching*, 1965. 30 × 35 cm. Collection of the artist.

550 S. MENTZ. *Drawing*, 1964. 53 × 50 cm. Collection of the artist.

551 M. BONOMI. *Conditional Freedom*, 1965. Wood-engraving in four colors, 130 × 103 cm. Collection: Philippe Guy Woog, Geneva.

552 D. BASILIO. *Cups, No. 1*, 1962. Etching and relief, 23 × 30 cm. Collection: M. G. Whittet, London.

553 S. CAMPOS MELLO. *Collage*, 1964. 45 × 60 cm. Collection of the artist.

554 P. CHAVES. *Elegy*, 1966. Relief with acrylic, 70 × 50 cm. Collection of the artist.

555 W. M. MORAIS, *Design II*, 1965. Engraving, relief, and printing inks on wood, 55 × 35 cm. Collection of the artist.

556 S. A. DE OLIVEIRA. *Drawing*, 1966. 70 × 50 cm. Collection of the artist.

557 M. H. ANDRES. *Drawing*, 1965. Charcoal, 60 × 70 cm. Collection of the artist.

558

559

560

561

562

563

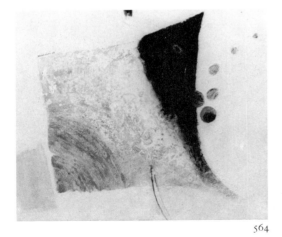

564

565

The influence of the Japanese artists must be taken into account, as well as the counter-influence that their group has received from Brazilian surroundings. The numerous Japanese colony in the state of São Paulo has produced some good artists who, joined by others from Japan, form a fairly compact group, known as Seibi. Some differences of formation and still more of tendency are nevertheless discernible, which shows that they are on the way to becoming assimilated in the general Brazilian culture. The chief exponent of the Seibi group is M. Mabe, whose earlier landscape

themes, which still showed signs of his oriental origins, have been gradually transformed into Abstractism—in accordance with the prevailing fashion. The most gifted of the group is Tomie Ohtake.

558 ITO. *Heuristica*, 1966. Wood, height 80 cm. Collection: Akemi Kishida, São Paulo.
559 FUKUSHIMA. Painting, 1964. Oil on canvas, 137 × 66 cm. Private collection, São Paulo.
560 BIN KONDO. *Tale*, 1965. Oil on canvas, 110 × 80 cm. Collection of the artist.

561 YO YOSHITOME. *Dramaturgy*, 1965. Oil on canvas, 145 × 151 cm. Collection of the artist.
562 J. K. SUZUKI. *Gouache*, 1963. 49 × 33.5 cm. Collection of the artist.
563 Y. TOYOTA. Group of paintings in the artist's studio, 1964.
564 WAKABAYASHI. *Design*, 1965. Indian ink and plastic emulsion on canvas, 110 × 128 cm. Collection: Niomar Muniz Sodré Bittencourt, Rio.
565 F. SHIRO. *Souk-el-arba*, 1965. Oil on canvas, 120 × 192 cm. Collection of the artist.

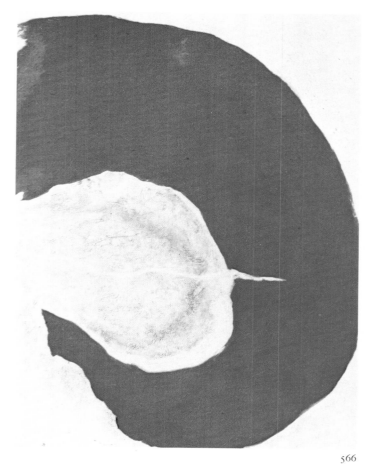

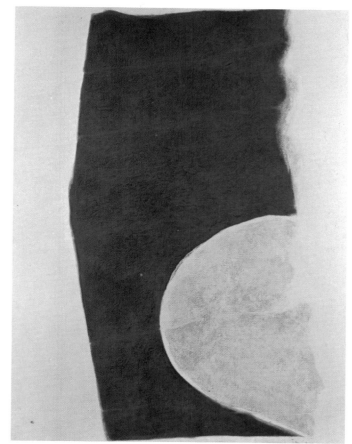

566

567

566 T. OHTAKE. *Red Painting*, 1967. Oil on canvas, 156 × 117 cm. Collection of the artist.
567 T. OHTAKE. *Painting*, 1965. Oil on canvas, 155 × 117 cm. Collection of the artist.
568 M. MABE. *Rio Landscape*, 1954. Oil on canvas, 60 × 80 cm. Private collection, São Paulo.
569 M. MABE. *Forms*, 1965. Oil on canvas, 160 × 160 cm. Collection of the artist.

568

569

570 Popular advertising in the outskirts of São Paulo: houses and building lots for sale.

Mass communication

Appealing to Freud, of whom they have read little, or to popular idols, probably on the way out, or in the name of revolutions, still to come in, the 'visual operators' in the graphic arts, even the best of them, are primarily concerned with getting their message across to the great majority of the consuming public—or, better still, to the whole of the consuming public, to the entire population.

To achieve this they use the most efficient means and do not disdain any kind of unusual stimulant, from sex, veiled only sufficiently to avoid prosecution, to the strong-man type of male dominance in all its degrees up to the conqueror of space. The phenomenon is world-wide; when it reached Brazil it was welcomed, absorbed, and soon became a normal feature of the nation's life.

There was some sporadic reaction. In about 1950 it was realized that all the advertising matter in newspapers, in magazines, and in the streets was, both artistically and psychologically, in pure North American style, and it was proposed to establish a Publicity School founded on national principles—and even on national errors—with the idea of promoting the diffusion of images to the masses that would be more improving to the mind and more attuned to local tastes and desires. It had little effect owing to the influence of the branches of the big New York publicity agencies.

All the same, some graphic artists have tried to effect an improvement, but their cure has sometimes turned out to be only another disease, as in the case of 'Ulmism', a malady brought back by artists who had been to Ulm and wanted to introduce the climate of Europe's icy mountains to the Tropic of Capricorn.

At present an attempt is being made to follow a course midway between these two extremes which, while giving due consideration to purity of layout, makes use of local subjects, forms, expressions, and surroundings. So far it has been practically limited to office calendars and a few pages of magazines intended for the cultured minority rather than the mass consumer. Even the publishers have been indifferent to the question: they go on having their book covers designed by artists who dash off sketches devoid of any significant message.

A modern source of aesthetic influence not to be disparaged comes from household electric appliances, whose strictly functional purposes impose foreign forms of design that are both pleasing and up to date and cannot be greatly modified. Yet one can often see these bright and rational objects in a house alongside dull furniture in rustic colonial or pseudo-antique styles.

Everything depends on the pressure of publicity. The masses think with the brains of the big industrialists and their respective sales departments. The sales promoter, in his press advertisements or on television, speaks to his victims in the familiar form of address (*tu*) in a country where usage still demands the polite third-person form. Our sociologists have still to tackle the problems of communication in an industrial society; in fact, they have never given us any general theory of Brazilian society at all.

As may be imagined, there are here, as elsewhere, at least two contrasting tendencies: the national and the international. The former is based on cultural tribalism; but a country in contact with the civilized world must not—in fact, cannot—isolate itself from international exchanges. Frontiers are vague and transient things. Brazil is busy finding out for herself just where she stands in the world of art: the young and the very young are enthusiastically clarifying their positions by means of exhibitions at Rio and São Paulo such as 'Opinião 65' and 'Proposta 65', which were rich in ideas and will certainly have had their effect on mass communication. One tendency is already clearly established: the rejection of ivory-tower art in favor of art that can be sold in the supermarkets. Another tendency, more extreme, derives from certain of the very latest theorists, and has to do with the 'alienation of art'.

571

572

573

574

576

575

577

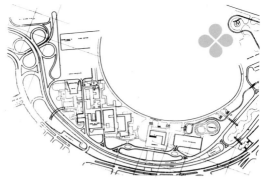

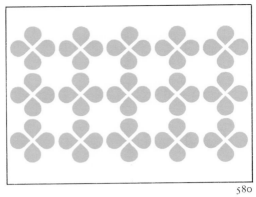

578

579

580

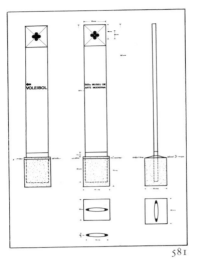

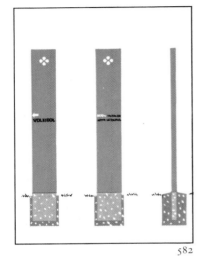

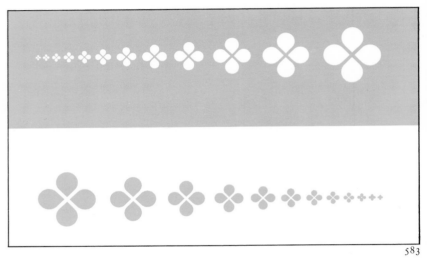

581

582

583

584

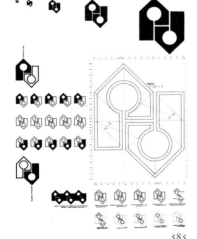

585

A. WOLLNER. Signposting of roads on the seafront esplanade at Rio de Janeiro, 1966:
578 Signpost.
579 Area of the signposting scheme: the quatrefoil emblem is derived from the cloverleaf intersection.
580 Repetition of the emblem.
581 and 582 Signpost drawings.
583 Reduction of the emblem.
584 WILLYS DE CASTRO and H. BARSOTTI. Manufacturer's mark for a mass-production furniture firm, Mobília Contemporânea, 1964.
585 A. SANOVICZ. Development of the symbol for the Joinville City Plan, 1965.

586 R. MARTINS. Development of the symbol of the ICOMI company, 1966. The company holds the mining concession in Amapá, the Federal Territory north of the Amazon, the form of whose boundaries was the starting point of the design.
Book and magazine covers:
587 Cover of *Senhor*, by Jaguar, 1960.
588 *Teoria da poesia concreta*, 1966.
589 Cover of *Contigo*, 1966.
590 'Brasil '66', cover of special number of *Direção* by S. V. da Silva, 1966.
591 *Cartas a meu pai*, by Kafka, cover by J. Cortez.
592 Cover of *Realidade*, 1966.

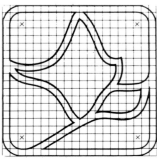

586

587

588

589

590

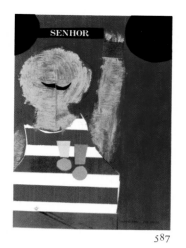

591

592

593

594

595

596

597

598

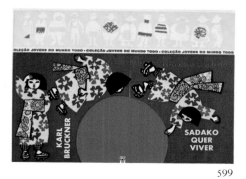

599

600

601

593 Catalogue *Maria Carmen*. Museum of Art, São Paulo, 1965.
594 Cover of *Claudia*, 1966. Photo by L. Parrella.
595 *Fui, vi e ... gostei!*, book cover by P. V. de Morais, 1966.

596 *Rosamundo e os outros*, book cover by Jaguar, 1966.
597 *A Viola do Diabo*, book cover by L. Bandeira, 1964.
598 *L'Enfance à la gorge*, book cover by S. Esmeraldo, 1965.

599 *Sadako quer viver*, book cover by O. Toscano.
600 Catalogue *II Exposição do Jovem Desenho Nacional*, 1966. Design by D. Ferrari.
601 *In Person at EL MATADOR*, LP record cover by Wesley Duke Lee, 1965.

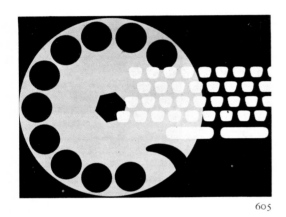

PERTURBAÇÕES INTESTINAIS

N PERTURBAÇÕES INTESTINAIS F

EN FÓF

SEN FÓRI

ISEN FÓRI

DISEN FÓRM

DISENFÓRMIO

602

PORQUE
PAGAR MAIS POR UM MOTOR
ABERTO ?

603

Confesse:
você sempre
teve um
certo mêdo
de entrar
na Casa Vogue,
não teve?

requinte é
sempre
VOGUE

604

605

606

602 D. PIGNATARI and R. MARTINS. Advertisement for a bowel astringent, Disenfórmio, 1962. The name of the complaint is graphically squeezed out of existence by the all-conquering letters of the name of the medicine.
603 Advertisement for Arno electric motors, 1966.
604 A. CHUST. Advertisement for a dress-shop, 1965. Idea and copy by Dulce Carneiro; agency, Panam, São Paulo.
605 Siemens advertisement from *Visão*, 1966.

606 Voith advertisement from *Visão*, 1966. Agency, Publitec.
607 Cover of Rhodia Moda brochure, 1966. Layout by L. de Almeida; photo by L. C. Autuori; agency, Standard Propaganda, São Paulo.
608 A. PERISSINOTO and A. MIHAINOVICH. Advertisement, 1965. Copy-writer, H. Dammann; agency, Alcantara Machado, São Paulo.
609 J. J. DE SOUZA. Advertisement, 1965. Copy-writer, N. Ferreira; realization, D. Branco; agency, Standard Propaganda, São Paulo.

Jóia/Julho sensacional!

NÚMERO ESPECIAL INGLATERRA!

Viaje
conosco
até Londres,
em Jóia
de julho!

607

não vá à Fenit
não vá à Fenit
não vá à Fenit

vai sim,
vai sim,
não seja
bôba

VIII FENIT
o maior mercado
têxtil do
hemisfério sul

de 14 a 29 de agôsto
Ibirapuera - São Paulo
Patrocinio : Sindicato da Indústria de
Fiação e Tecelagem
em Geral no Estado de São Paulo
Promoção : Alcantara Machado
Comércio e Empreendimentos

608

— O Serviço Secreto
de Sua Majestade
ainda não descobriu
como Saméllo conseguiu obter o
modêlo autêntico
da botina de
James Bond.

SAMÉLLO

609

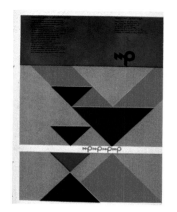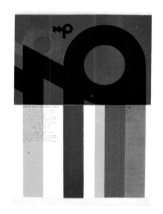

610

O QUE É QUE SE FAZ COM UM PAI NO **DIA DO PAPAI?**

Você pode levá-lo ao Jardim Zoológico. Ou à praia para ver as ondulações (afinal, os pais nunca foram tão jovens). Você pode domesticar uns passarinhos para fazerem em volta dêle uma revoada de amor. E você pode pegar o dinheiro (dêle, é claro) e lhe oferecer um presente mágico e portátil: a

Lettera 22

olivetti

Olivetti Industrial s.a.
sede: São Paulo
fábrica: Guarulhos (S.P.)
filiais, agentes exclusivos e revendedores,
em todo o território nacional.

611

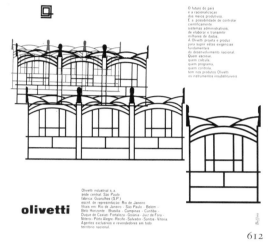

O futuro do país
e a racionalização
dos meios produtivos.
É a possibilidade de controlar
cientificamente
sistemas administrativos,
de elaborar e transmitir
milhares de dados.
A Olivetti projeta e produz
para suprir estas exigências
fundamentais
do desenvolvimento nacional.
Quem escreve,
quem calcula,
quem programa,
quem controla,
tem nos produtos Olivetti
os instrumentos insubstituíveis.

olivetti

Olivetti industrial s.a.
sede central: São Paulo
fábrica: Guarulhos (S.P.)
escrit. de representação: Rio de Janeiro
filiais em: Rio de Janeiro - São Paulo - Belém -
Belo Horizonte - Brasília - Campinas - Curitiba -
Duque de Caxias - Fortaleza - Goiana - Juiz de Fora -
Niterói - Pôrto Alegre - Recife - Salvador - Santos - Vitória
Agentes exclusivos e revendedores em todo
território nacional.

612

613

614

610 Projects for a publicity campaign for factory machinery designed by A. Chust, 1965. Agency, Panam, São Paulo.
611 Olivetti advertisement by M. Fernandes, 1966.
612 Olivetti advertisement by B. Buffoni, 1966.
613 Photograph used in an advertisement by M. Guarnieri for Duratex, São Paulo, 1966. Agency, Lince Propaganda, São Paulo.
614 B. BUFFONI. Decorative panel, 1960, for Olivetti Industrial S.A., São Paulo.

129

615

616

617

We must remind ourselves here once again that there are two coexistent but clearly separate trends in graphic communication: the popular, with its ever vital inventiveness, and the professional, which increasingly tends to take on international forms. The autonomy of the northeast in this field is almost inevitable, and the artists there make full use of the native folk-lore and popular expressiveness. In the south, where industrialization is the outward sign of progress, publicity tends to assume North American forms, yet with some admixture of Brazilian elements.

618

619

620

621

622

623

624

615 Cover of the catalogue of an exhibition of painters at Natal, 1965.

616 Poster for the 'Atelier + 10' group of artists, Recife.

617 Cobbler's sign at Diadema, São Paulo, 1967.

618 Road sign at Diadema.

619 Baker's sign and other street advertisements, Diadema.

620 Poster for the Rhodia Moda 'Brazilian Fashion Team', 1966. Layout by J. Ferreira Filho; agency, Standard Propaganda, São Paulo.

621 ZIRALDO. Poster for the First International Festival of the Popular Song, Rio, 1966.

622 M. GONÇALVES. Playbill for a production of Staircase by Charles Dyer at the Teatro Princesa Isabel, Rio, 1967.

623 L. GRINOVER. Commercial Christmas greetings card, 1966.

624 JAGUAR. Subscription blank for the magazine Senhor, 1963.

625 Pharmaceutical packaging by MetRo 3, 1967.
626 Pharmaceutical pack varied according to country of sale, by MetRo 3.
627 Philips advertisement.
628 Advertisement by MetRo 3, 1967.
629 Double-page Ford advertisement by MetRo 3.
630 Poster for cinema festival held at the Faculty of Architecture, University of São Paulo, 1966.
631 Gessy Lever advertisement (children's art competition), 1966.

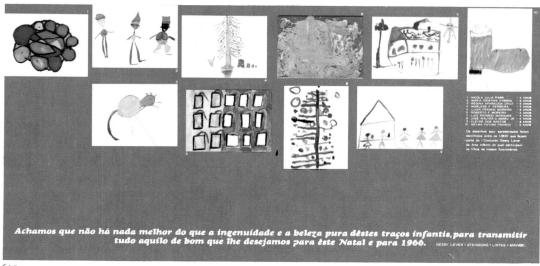

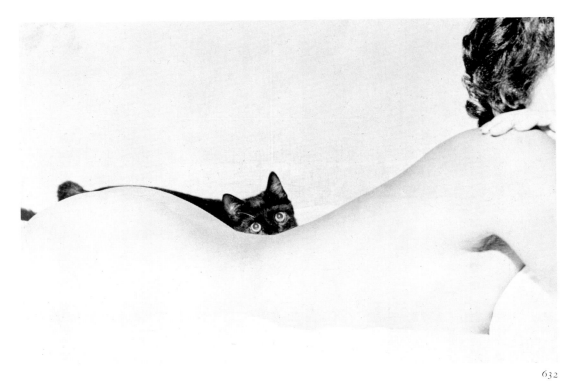

632

633

634

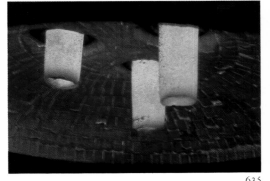

635

636

637

638

Photography is still somewhat behindhand. Yet it is an activity that is of fundamental importance today, for it is largely through the camera that we receive our first impressions of all the other arts, and we depend on it for our knowledge of artistic activity throughout the world—not to mention the fact that as an art form in its own right it should be the perfect expression of an age that has been called the 'civilization of the image'. In the big urban centers such as Rio and São Paulo one finds groups of a hundred or so practitioners in each of the various fields of architecture, graphic design, interior design, fashions, theater, and so on, who exchange ideas among themselves, maintain standards, and more or less determine the prevailing styles; but nothing like this seems to take place among the photographers, who therefore lack the incentives that belonging to such groups provides. A certain technical proficiency has been reached in press photography, especially sport; but photographers who can produce good work outside the movement confined to pictorial illustration, which, as in the case of the uninhibited adepts of neo-realism, tends to use the photograph as the best means of revealing social realities, are rare indeed.

632 S. HARNISCH. *Nude with Cat*, 1950.
633 C. ANDUJAR. *Light Effects*, 1964.
634 J. MEDEIROS. *Macumba*, 1960.
635 JOÃO XAVIER. *Furnace*, 1963.
636 L. BRAGA. *'Babá alapalá': Egun (ghost) of Oxalá dancing* (evocation of the dead during a *macumba* ritual), 1960.
637 M. BISILLIAT. *Body*, 1964.
638 S. STUPAKOFF. *Mother and Son*, 1963.
639 M. A. VIGLIOLA. *Manikin*, 1964.

639

640

641

642

Dresses designed by A. Penna for Rhodia Moda and shown at fashion parades abroad in 1967:

640 Muslin tunic over a satin dress made by Cori (left), and a dress in crêpe-georgette made by Tomaso (right), photographed in Paris.

641 Dress made of feathers by Sabrina (left), and a dress of black sequins (right), photographed at Maxim's in Paris.

642 Evening dress made by Tomaso, material designed by F. Geelmuyden, photographed at Julien's in Paris.

643 Tunic dress in organdie made by Tomaso, photographed in the Hotel Solvay, Brussels.

644 Pajamas with separate blouse made by Carillon from material designed by H. Barsotti, photographed in Paris with objects from the collection of Robert S. Walker.

645 House-pajamas made by the Atelier Parisiense from printed material designed by L. Jasmin, photographed in the Güell Park, Barcelona.

643

644

645

646 Dresses designed by A. Penna for Rhodia Moda, 1966.
647 Ready-made model by M. Gorovitz, 1966.
648 Models presented by Rhodia Moda in a fashion parade in London, 1966. Materials designed by F. de Lemos and A. Martins, models by A. Penna.

646

647

648

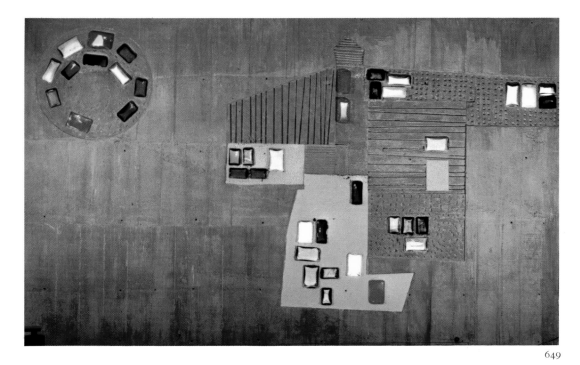

649

650

651

652

653

649 J. W. TOSCANO. Interior wall decoration in wood and glazed tiles, São Paulo, 1966.

650 E. NOBELING. Vase, 1965. Ceramic. Collection: Edith Landmann, São Paulo.

651 R. SASSON. Outside wall in glazed tiles, São Paulo, 1967.

652 F. BONDI. Decoration, 1967. Rock crystal, granite, topaz, marble, and glaze, 22 × 9 cm.

653 A. CARELLI. Outside mosaic pavement, 32 sq.m., São Paulo, 1967.

654 CARYBÉ. End-wall of a building, concrete, 15 × 5 m. Salvador, 1966.

655 Designs for decorative paving, São Paulo.

654

655

656

657

658

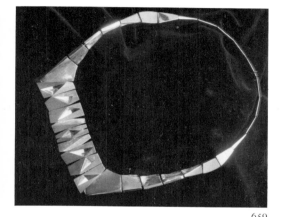

659

660

661

662

663

664

665

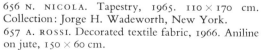

656 N. NICOLA. Tapestry, 1965. 110 × 170 cm.
Collection: Jorge H. Wadeworth, New York.

657 A. ROSSI. Decorated textile fabric, 1966. Aniline
on jute, 150 × 60 cm.

658 F. BRENNAND. *Vase of Flowers*, 1964. Tapestry
woven by the Atelier M. R., São Paulo.

659 R. E. LEVI. Necklace, 1965. Executed in gold by
A. R. Moreno.

660 J. DOUCHEZ. *Aquarius*, 1966. Tapestry, 108 × 160
cm. Collection: Edgard F. Kaiser, New York.

661 R. SASSON. Necklace of gold nuggets attached to
white-gold links, 1967.

662 C. MOURÃO. Necklace in chased silver with
natural onyx center-piece, 1964.

663 R. BURLE MARX. Necklace in gold and semi-
precious stones, 1966.

664 L. ZANOTTO. Brooch in gold and silver, 1966.

665 and 667 P. CORRÊA DE ARAUJO. Necklaces in
silver and pearls, and silver and semi-precious stones,
1966.

666 L. BO. Necklace of aquamarines set in gold, 1947.

666

667

All objects used for the same purpose and produced at the same time will obviously bear some resemblance to each other, so it is not much use trying to trace origins or recognize schools. The canons of industrial design put a further restriction upon the fluctuations of taste and the search for novelty; they impose unification and purity of form almost to the point of geometrical perfection, until the only alternative left is between the sphere and the cube, the choice depending on whether rotundity or angularity is the prevailing fashion. Brazil has entered this field rather late, already influenced by imported goods, and with the development of her own industries has had to start from the basis of established foreign forms, American rather than European.

671

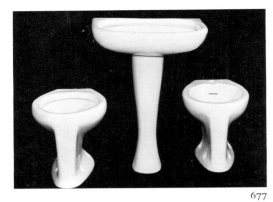

677

672

673

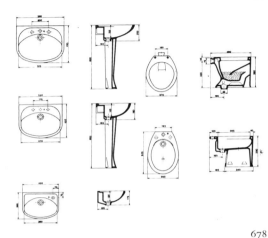

678

668   669

679

674   675

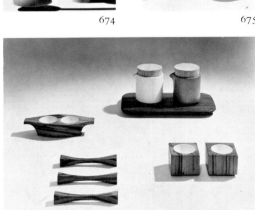

676

680

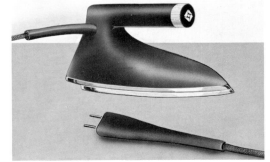

681

670

668 E. DOMINICI. Desk lamp adjustable for height, shade in blue acrylic, metal parts in brass and chromium, 1966.

669 M. MONTE. Reading lamp in jacarandá and silver, 1966.

670 M. MONTE. Casseroles in ceramic.

671 and 672 G. LIZARRAGA. Two sets of glasses, 1965. Manufactured by San Marco, São Paulo.

673 THE R. BAERLEIN GROUP. Jacarandá rack with three stainless-steel holders for colored glass herb jars with cork stoppers, 10 × 30 cm.

674 THE R. BAERLEIN GROUP. Candlesticks in spray-painted wood.

675 THE R. BAERLEIN GROUP. Ashtrays, height 39 cm.

676 M. MONTE. Tableware in jacaradá: tray with cork-stoppered ceramic cruets, pepper and salt cellars, knife-rests.

677 and 678 Design Department of the Ideal-Standard company, São Paulo. Articles of bathroom porcelain ware, 1965.

679 L. GRINOVER. Fluorescent desk lamp, 1966, in painted metal with acrylic diffuser, manufactured by Noviform, São Paulo.

680 and 681 R. MARTINS. Electric iron designed for the Prima Eletro Domésticos company, São Paulo, 1966. The novel feature is the fusion of handle and casing into a single element, so reducing the number of components and making the iron easier to manage.

682 L. BO. Two-piece easy chair with adjustable seat, in plastic, metal, and foam rubber.

683 S. R. RODRIGUES. Auditorium seats, in wood and leather, 1965. Made by Oca, Rio.

684 S. R. RODRIGUES. 'Soft' chair, in wood, leather, and foam rubber, 1957. Made by Oca, Rio. Can be taken to pieces.

682

683

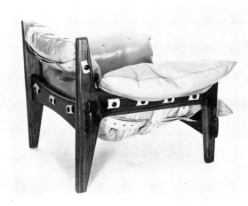

684

685

686

687

688

689

690

691

685 L. BO. Auditorium seats for the Museum of Modern Art, Salvador, 1960. In standardized elements of wood and leather designed for hand manufacture and to be taken apart and reassembled as required.
686 MAUD GROUP. Chair in wood and upholstery, 1966.
687 M. ARNOULT and N. WESTWATER. Chair, 1964. Made by Mobília Contemporânea, São Paulo.
688 N. WESTWATER. Nesting chairs in tubular steel and formica, 1965.
689 A. L. PONTUAL, in collaboration with R. Cruz Vargas, P. Pontual, and A. Facioli. Swivel-chair, 1962.
690 MAUD GROUP. Chair, in wood, leather, and foam rubber, 1966.
691 G. DE BARROS. Superimposable beds in wood, mortised and tenoned, 1965. Made by Objeto, São Paulo.

Our survey so far has been concerned, on the whole, with what we have called civilized art, using the term in a wide sense and admitting some exceptions. We now proceed to a rapid review of what in actual fact are the artistic standards of the general mass of consumers. We must insist again upon the distinction to be made between the quality of the popular product as found in the interior of the country, and the articles that are produced for the big cities. The difference between them is fundamental: on the one hand, the repetition of traditional styles is accepted in everything; on the other, there is a demand for the products of stylists, generally educated abroad, who claim to be in line with the latest international taste.

Take furniture to begin with. One can imagine the simplicity of the old colonial interiors which, though in line with European styles, were conditioned by the frugality and simplicity of the early settlers. But with the rise of the middle classes the demands of ostentation brought great changes, which reached the height of absurdity in the middle of the nineteenth century. Eça de Queiroz, in his well-known social observations, remarked: 'The old simple usages were scornfully abandoned: every man sought to get himself a baron's coronet, and at well over 100 in the shade the ladies were content to liquefy under woolen cloth and rich velvets. In the houses there was no longer to be found an honest rush-seated chair in which, at the end of the day, the body might find rest and coolness; garish damasks began to appear, furniture with gilt claw-legs, beribboned curtains, and all the stuffiness of upholstery, which may keep out the cold in Paris or London but lets the germs lie snug and cosy.' This state of affairs is still not altogether superseded, and the interior decorators favored by the middle classes continue to beribbon and upholster the rich houses. A sampling of taste in furniture, based on *Casa e Jardim* ('House and Garden'), a periodical addressed to middle class readers, gave the following results. The 110-page issue examined (December 1965) contained 215 illustrations, of which illustrations of strictly modern styles (such as those illustrated in this book), numbered 62 in the advertisements and 14 in the text; illustrations of antique or antique-inspired styles, 21 in the advertisements and 68 in the text; illustrations of hybrid styles (mixed modern and antique), 1 on the cover, 27 in the advertisements, and 22 in the text.

Ever since the war an immense effort has been directed at the middle-class psyche in Brazil in order to impose the acceptance of new industrial products, and in 1964 about 60 million dollars were spent on advertising, almost all allotted to visual campaigns. The mass of the public, including the country people, has therefore come to accept rational design in furniture, in household electric appliances, and, in fact, in commercial products in general. Market researchers and other investigators have thus come to the conclusion that in Brazil, too, a mass civilization is in process of being formed that will be increasingly exacting about the aesthetic element. One indication of this is the popularity of rational, modern furniture, which has increased rapidly, though partly, perhaps, because it is cheaper. Faced with this, the richer classes have instinctively reacted by going in for romantic styles and elevating the old colonial furniture to the height of current fashion.

692

693

694

692 J. ZALSZUPIN. Office furniture, 1966: desk in solid jacarandá with cork-faced panels; swivel-chair with solid jacarandá base, leather upholstery. On the wall behind, paintings by F. Petit (left) and J. M. Zaragoza.

693 M. ARNOULT. Series of desks in separable parts, 1965.

694 A. MAGNELLI. Office furniture in tubular steel, wood, and leather, 1966. Made by Tecnogeral, São Paulo.

695 and 696 View and plan of the Olivetti Brasiliana stand for displaying the model Tecno 3 electric type-writer at the Domestic Utilities Fair, São Paulo, 1967. The plan of the route followed by the visitor forms the firm's mark; he first enters a space with warm air-conditioning and an artificially produced clatter of conventional typewriters and then passes, with a sense of relief, into the cool, silent atmosphere of the section in which the new electric model is displayed. Realization by P. M. Bardi and W. D. Lee.

697 and 698 J. C. CAUDURO. Joint for tubular steel assemblies to support exhibition panels, 1964.

699 and 700 J. C. CAUDURO. Display of products of the Villares company at the Engineering Fair, São Paulo, 1966.

701 Street decorations for the Rio Carnival, 1966.

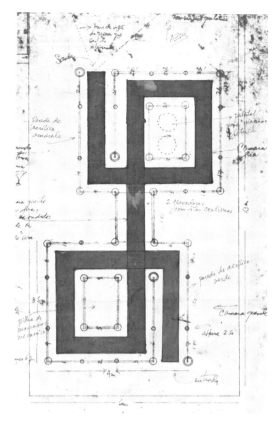

695

696

697

698

699

700

701

702

703

704

705

706

707

708

709

710

711

The Brazilian theater has its own history. During the XVII and XVIII centuries it was largely religious in nature having been initiated by the Orders. An interesting type of romanticism developed during the past century, but it is in this century, especially after the war, that vivacity and originality have become incorporated in Brazilian drama. These pages offer an idea of the work of Brazilian artists in the field of scenography.

702 M. GONÇALVES. Stage setting for *Victor, ou les enfants au pouvoir* by Roger Vitrac, Teatro Novo, Rio, 1963.
703 B. PAES LEME. Setting and costumes for *Auto da Alma* by Gil Vicente, Teatro do Conservatorio, Rio, 1965.
704 Scene from *Vida e morte de Severina* by J. Cabral de Melo Neto, which took the first prize at the Festival of the University Theater at Nancy in 1966.
705 Setting for *Stone Angel* by Tennessee Williams, Teatro Brasileiro de Comedia, São Paulo, 1959.

706 and 707 F. IMPERIO. Settings for *Andorra* by Max Frisch, Teatro Oficina, São Paulo, 1964.
708 Scene from *Caligula* by Camus, Teatro Castro Alves, Salvador, 1961. Scenery and costumes by L. Bo.
709 and 710 Setting and scene from Brecht's *Drei-Groschen-Oper*, Teatro Castro Alves, Salvador, 1961. Scenery by L. Bo, costumes by Beatriz Tanaka.
711 Scene from *Vida e morte de Severina* by J. Cabral de Melo Neto, Theater of the Catholic University of São Paulo, 1961.

143

712 H. EICHBAUER. Setting for Chekov's *The Cherry Orchard*, 1966.
713 H. EICHBAUER. Setting for Gorky's *Vasa Geleznova*, 1966.
714 H. EICHBAUER. Setting for *The Cherry Orchard*, 1966.
715 H. EICHBAUER. Design for a setting, 1966.
716 H. EICHBAUER. Setting for Molière's *Les Précieuses ridicules*, 1965.

712

713

714

715

716

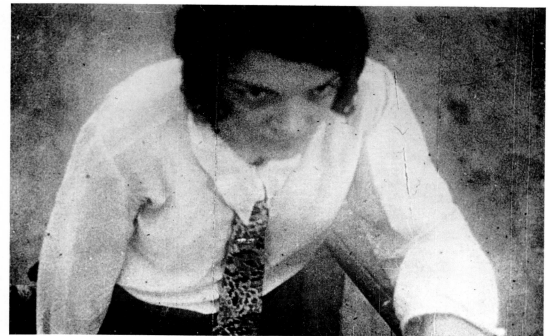

717 Still from *Limite*, 1933, by Mario Peixoto.

The new cinema

The Brazilian cinema achieved a certain notoriety in Europe when awards were given at the Cannes Festival to a new type of commercialized western about the *cangaceiros* of the northeast. These half real, half legendary outlaws appear in the literature of the so-called northern novel by such writers as José Lins do Rego and Jorge Amado, which describe the wretched social conditions due, in the past, to the struggle against colonial oppression and the rapacity of the landowners, and still close to starvation owing to a tragically unpredictable climate with its severe droughts and sudden destructive floods. But the modest history of the Brazilian cinema goes farther back than the onset of this new wave. The isolated experiments of the principal director of the silent film, H. Mauro, who was active in the state of Minas Gerais between 1925 and 1933, are of remarkable importance, and are comparable with the rise of modernism in painting and with the music of Villa-Lobos, with whom, incidentally, Mauro produced *O Descobrimento do Brasil*.

Typical of the genuine, primitive Brazilian, with all the resource of the pioneer, he would do all the jobs of director, actor, cameraman, scenarist, himself, yet manage to produce, with the most rudimentary equipment, a film like *Ganga bruta*, a true masterpiece, now revered as a famous prototype by the new school of cinematographers. But the real triumph was a film called *Limite* made in 1933 by a youth called Mario Peixoto and shown at the Marble Arch Pavilion Club in

London, where it ran for two months. It was seen by Eisenstein, who devoted a long article to it in which he declared that Peixoto had a 'film-mind', an extraordinary sense of visual rhythm, and a 'very individual idiom', and continued: 'By this act of selection the artist appropriates a corner of the universe, isolates it through the camera-eye, and puts into the space something also of himself. In all ages it is the consciously assumed positions that leave marks that cannot be erased with the passing of the centuries. And such is the quality of this film. I am convinced that twenty years from now it will still throb with fresh vitality, as rich in film structure as it is today: poetic and bitter at the same time, but already deeply rooted, pitifully born mature, like something that has had no childhood.'

Limite was never released for general exhibition, it has vanished from circulation, and its creator no longer takes any interest in the cinema. There followed a long period of inactivity until, after the war, a cinema school was included in the organization of the Museum of Art, São Paulo, which counted much on Alberto Cavalcanti, the well-known Brazilian film-director who had emigrated to Europe in his youth, and who was invited to return to Brazil. To him is due the establishment of a film industry that was something more than an affair of amateurs: first-class technicians were called in, studios built, suitable equipment imported, and a group of young film workers was formed. He built up the national cinema—but with too much European zest to find appreciation in uncomprehending circles

which, as he put it, were full of 'dishonest and ignorant' people who needed to be got rid of. As it turned out, he was got rid of himself: a year or two later, after more argument than work, he returned to Paris, leaving behind him a few good films such as *Simão o Caolho*, 1952, and *O Canto do mar*, 1954. The latter, a transformation into Brazilian terms of his old *En rade* of 1927, shows his technical ability but also reveals that he had not altogether found his bearings in the new geographical and ethnographical surroundings. His last film was a tragedy of love among rich victims of tuberculosis, which moved more to laughter than to tears.

After the period of the Vera Cruz productions there was a phase of the usual type of speculative enterprise undertaken with the hope of profits but with little artistic or administrative seriousness. Attempts at Rio and São Paulo, though they had the services of foreign would-be film experts, especially Italians, many of whom claimed to have worked with Rossellini but who, when put to the test, were found to be mere incompetents, ended in failure. The one man to save his reputation was the Brazilian Lima Barreto, who had the temperament of the romantic novelist and made *O Cangaceiro* in 1954, but has since disappeared. He was followed in the genre by the actor Anselmo Duarte, who made *Pagador de promessas*, which received an award at Cannes in 1964, as *O Cangaceiro* had previously. Some foreign companies produced films which, apart from their hamhandedness, were rich only in their appeal to the baser and stupider instincts, yet

718 A. Cavalcanti during the making of *O Canto do mar*, 1954.

they were highly praised by the critics, who, like those of the plastic arts, are anything but severe. Meanwhile, at Salvador, a group of young enthusiasts has begun to turn again to the rudimentary methods of H. Mauro and M. Peixoto with films of the stories of the northeast. Far away from the big cities, these irregulars have no need of studios, lighting, smiling stars, amateur financiers full of self-importance; only a camera and cameraman, some film, actors found on the spot, and freedom from advisers and bosses. It is this individualistic cinema, which takes a stand against industrialization of the art, that is gaining ground. Salvador, the capital of the state of Bahia, a city regarded as the Mecca of historical rhetoric and folk-lore for tourists, has recently begun to consider the question of art by establishing the Museum of Modern Art, and it is in this center that the young film-makers have started what is already known as the Bahia school.

It was thus, and due especially to the initiative of G. Rocha, that the New Cinema, whose real concern, like that of the early Italian Neo-realism, is with social protest rather than the telling of a story, had its origin. There is no difficulty in perceiving the ideological slant. The films are a kind of diary of the conscience, full of the revolutionary's heartfelt generosity. The intention of their producers is to make known the real facts of a country that is faced with immense social problems that will soon have to be solved. The seventh art is the only one that is drawing attention to the two faces of society.

Of course, not all the present Brazilian cinema is 'new'; what still predominates is the commercialism of the film for ostriches who bury their heads to avoid seeing the truth, and who see the nation only as the two big cities where everything proceeds, well or ill, for the best. However, in these last few years, the young film-makers have also attempted to probe the social problems of the cities by means of documentary themes, though not yet openly attacking the anomalies peculiar to rapid urban development which tends to upset the ethnological balance. The Brazilian cinema is still in a primitive stage and is only making its first contacts with the generation that will have to shoulder the responsibility for finding the political equilibrium on which the stability of the country depends. For the moment, it has been said, the New Cinema is only the announcement of a programme, and it is not yet possible to see how it will turn out; for there are already signs of a certain disaccord between the intentions of the film-makers and what the public wants to see in the picture theaters. The public, in fact, has only a limited appetite for the representation of social parables.

The revelation of so much poverty, distress, and superstition serves admirably to make the point, but the argument, as argument, is nearly always crudely, sometimes hysterically, expressed, and it all weighs on the negative side of the scale. In all the dark and grim scene there is no hint of where to turn to get a breath of fresh air. The young film-makers have still to discover that there is some work of social improvement going on in Brazil today, such as hydro-electric schemes, trunk roads through miles of virgin forest, the new capital, steelworks, universities, and—last but not least—the wide diffusion of the automobile, which is acquiring more symbolic significance than the old branch of the coffee-plant. There is material here no less spectacular than that of the northern novel.

719

720

721

722

723

724

725

726

727

728

729

730

719 *Pagador de promessas*, 1964. Director, A. Duarte.

720 *Bahia de Todos os Santos*, 1961. Director, Trigueirinho Neto.

721 *Vidas sêcas*, 1962, from the novel by Graciliano Ramos. Director, N. Pereira dos Santos.

722 *São Paulo Sociedade Anónima*, 1964, Director, L. S. Person.

723 and 724 *A Hora e a volta de Augusto Madraga*, 1966. Director, R. Santos; producer, L. C. Barreto.

725 *Esta noite encarnarei o teu cadaver*, 1966. Horror film made with live snakes and spiders. Director, J. Mojica.

726 *Desafio*, 1966. Director, P. C. Saraceni.

727 *Deus e o Diabo na terra do sol*, 1963. Director, G. Rocha.

728 *Nossa escola de samba*, 1966. Documentary directed by M. Giménez.

729 and 730 *Terra em transe*, 1967. Director, G. Rocha.

731 Teenage fanaticism in the Hall of the Municipal Council of São Paulo for the pop singer Roberto Carlos, 1966. The painting on the wall is of St Paul, the city's patron saint.

The beat of music

This profile cannot be concluded without something being said about music, which of all the arts is perhaps closest to the Brazilians' modes of feeling and expression. Although it has been involved in the same historical events we have mentioned in speaking of the plastic arts, it has had, perhaps, a less significant role, especially when we come to the avant-garde movements of the present century.

The first European settlers found an indigenous musical culture, which was both primitive and typical. The early missionaries, in order to achieve a more effective psychological penetration of the native mind for catechizing purposes, began to incorporate its rhythms in their liturgies and to turn them into Christian chants. When the Jesuits began producing their sacred dramas, or *autos*, the Indians were the innocent participators and singers, and used their own instruments and those brought from Europe by the priests. Meanwhile, the lay Portuguese were introducing their own types of music—*modas*, *solaus* and *serranilhas*, harmonic tones, strophic division—and instruments such as the guitar, as well as their dances, especially the typical *Bumba-meu-boi*, and the Spanish boleros, fandangos and tyrannas. These various influences were absorbed in mass by the Indians, who gave them automatic re-expression with the same results as they had brought about in Baroque decoration, where the hand of the native craftsman uncon-sciously distorted and modified the style and character of the original design.

Soon afterwards, with the coming of the African influx, the wail of the antiphon was superseded by the drums and rhythms of the negro dances, called *lundus*, the sounds of which were gradually given new form and spirit in the ebullience of the new ethnic environment. These forms of music differed from region to region, on account of the great distances between them, and from one type of community to another, especially in the cities, and still more in the cities of the north, where the Gregorian origins are still discernible today. It must have been music of melancholy rhythms and nostalgic songs, dealing mostly with the sadness and burden of life.

Into this first amalgam of innate and germinating elements, with its Afro-Iberian substratum (for nothing remained of the Indian culture, which had been discarded or swallowed up in the name of progress), there came the intrusion, in the eighteenth century, of new popular music and instruments from other regions and of fresh immigrant influences, and a certain cultural attainment was reached. Classical music, escaping from the severity of the Church, entered the scene in the first opera houses established at Salvador, Rio, and São Vicente, the harbor which later gave origin to the city of Santos. The Jesuits founded choir schools; craftsmen started to make musical instru-ments. In the state of Minas Gerais a school of Baroque church music flourished—the recently rediscovered *Barroco mineiro*. The patriarch of Brazilian music, José Maurício Nunes Garcia, composer of a celebrated Requiem, died in 1830; and the printing of scores, which began shortly after this date, led to a much wider diffusion of music. Opera had its greatest vogue at about the end of the century, and the arrival of powerful European influences in both popular and classical music brought still further enrichment. Brazil was to build up her passion for the art of sound, which was to become one of the manifestations of national unity, in somewhat the same manner as with football—by making it an occasion for popular merry-making.

The Americas, as importers of music, showed preferences that may be easily imagined. The musicologist Vasco Mariz notes that 'in 1887, the birth-year of Villa-Lobos, the large but select membership of the Beethoven Club or of the Society for Classical Concerts paid homage to the Piano Fantasia from the *Sonnambula*, went into ecstasies over the *Traviata*, and with stoical snobbishness put up with Bach'. It was the story of painting over again, when, after the Academy was set up by the King in 1816 and a mission of French artists imported, commemorative history painting was practised and the existence of Impressionism ignored; although isolated amateurs expressed their feelings in paint, neglected, and inspired only by rural simplicity and the events of everyday life. And so it was with the music of the people, who were ignorant of culture in the refined sense: music continued to be produced; the local heritage and contributions from outside were modified and received new expression with a natural ease that was quite capable of adapting an air of Boccherini to a samba. Musicians who aspired to create a national art turned their attention to an Indianizing romanticism, as the poets had done. Carlos Gomes, a not untalented follower of Verdi, made use of libretti exalting Indian legends; they represented an early hint of autonomy and corresponded to the immense compositions celebrating Brazilian history painted by Pedro Américo and Vítor Meirelles, but their inspiration was derivative, second-hand. Wagnerism found its disciples, as did culturalism: the young went to study at Milan, in the shadow of the Scala. Another Italianist was Henrique Oswald, an elegant and sentimental composer. Of true Brazilian inspiration there was perhaps only Alberto Nepomuceno, who harmonized the popular song with finer feeling and a clear style, yet without owing too much to Europe.

It is necessary to pass on to the century of the World Wars to find something new in intention or results. But even at the Week of Modern Art Villa-Lobos was mercilessly hissed by the audience, and was regarded seriously as a composer only by a few cultivators of good taste who were abreast of the latest ideas. He traveled the length and breadth of the country, listened to the voices of the jungle, and from the vast treasure-house of the music of the streets, of the seashore, of the fields he borrowed expressions—gay, typical, infinitely varied—of the land and the race for his compositions, which were, at last, Brazilian. They were sometimes chaotic, rough hewn and primitive, but he never entirely forgot the teaching of Bach. Mention should also be made of Glauco Velasquez, whose compositions were highly appreciated by Darius Milhaud when the latter resided in Rio; and of Jaime Ovalle, inspired by Afro-Brazilian folk-lore, and Luciano Gallet, a worthy respecter of tradition.

In the following generations various names were prominent in Brazilian music, representative of definite individual tendencies rather than any general manner, some having a distinct style: Camargo Guarnieri, Luís Cosme, José Batista Siquei-ra, Radames Gnattali, Francisco Mignone, Brasilio Itiberê, Heckel Tavares, José Vieira Brandão, Frutuoso Vianna—to name only the best known and among whom must not be forgotten Mário de Andrade, who was also a musicologist of proven worth. 'The messages transmitted by these composers', notes Mariz, 'are incompatible among themselves, be they well or ill delivered, but they are always attractive. Will there be a Brazilian composer, one day, who will unite the discordant voices and combine them in unison' and so bring into being a form of musical expression that will be spontaneously national? It is a question which prompts many doubts and reservations, and which might, indeed, be asked of all the arts we have been considering in this profile. Brahms, a German, expressed Hungarian emotions; Heandel represents English sentiments in spite of his nationality. The history of music is full of such a-nationalisms, and it may be asked if to insist on such matters may not be outdated in a world in which everything tends to one kind of mentality.

The Brazilian musicians of the generation born at the time of the First World War—Guerra-Peixe, Alceu Bocchino, Mario Tavares and Oswald Lacerda—have helped to give consistency to Brazilian music, but once again with marked differences between them. They sought to draw their inspiration from folk-lore, while younger groups, including, for instance, Claudio Santoro and Edino Krieger, no longer obey the precept to 'look for it at home' and aspire to internationalism, as the plastic arts have done. Among the most recent names: Carlos Nobre, Almeida Prado, the two Duprats, and Sergio Mendes. It is difficult to distinguish between art and craft, between real genius that will live in history and a facility for music, however versatile, that will survive only in the files of old newspapers. What might be termed craft music is highly active, generally with little theoretical grounding, but favored by a resonance that gives new form to the urge of the people to express themselves in terms of music. While the whole of this stream of music disappears while searching for its bed in the difficult country of international positions, the flood of popular music continues unabated, and even threatens to burst its banks.

The whole world is familiar with the outpouring of music released during the Brazilian carnivals, especially the Rio carnival, which is an incredible and riotous harvest of songs, marches, *frevos* of Pernambuco or Bahia, sambas, and numerous other forms of composition, one more lively and exciting than another, all frenzied, issuing from the underground source that taps the whole of Brazil, irrespective of topographical origin, something miraculously national, in the same way that the Portuguese language drove out all others but diverged from the language of Portugal in doing so. Into the melting-pot of Rio go the musical contributions of the entire country, to be relaunched, industrialized, upon the world through the new media of communication.

Every year the people reinvent the carnival ritual, which has been maturing during the intervening months, and anxiously await the few days of free existentialist explosion, the many-sided event with its numerous manifestations of art—spectacle, choreography, poetry, music, dance, satire, religious invocation—that takes place in collective intimacy. Five hundred editions of music were published for the carnival of 1966. The exuberance of this musical activity knows no restraint, and has even produced the secessionist movement known as the Bossa Nova led by Vinicius de Morais and Jobin, which represents something that transcends the traditional fashion (as has also happened in painting): a tendency to look beyond frontiers, to approach a style more easily accepted internationally yet without losing the tone of melancholy—in this case a very minor tone—that explains the success of the Bossa Nova abroad.

Radio and television, and especially the industry of the phonograph record, are affecting the purity and authenticity of the old popular music. Traditional song writers and singers such as Ary Barroso, Heitor dos Prazeres, Noel Rosa and Dorival Caymmi, are being succeeded in the public favor by such new stars as Roberto Carlos who, starting from the tradition of the Northeastern storytellers, has become a Beatles-like phenomenon—though of a different, home-grown type.

So the new popular music is pop, and by 1966 it had even entered the churches, drawing a strong reproof from the Archbishop of Curitiba who denounced a young people's Mass for being untraditional. All the same, this process of adaptation is gaining ground, as when the early missionaries found that they had to adapt the native music to the ends of Christianity.

General

Index

A

ABRAMO, Livio (1903, Araraquara, SP) – Engraver and teacher. Owns a perfect technique on woodcutting. Lives in Assunción, Paraguay. 37, 111

ADAMI, Hugo (1900, São Paulo, SP) – Painter. 37

AGUILAR, José Roberto (1941, São Paulo, SP) – Painter. 89

ALEIJADINHO, nickname of Antônio Francisco Lisbôa (1738, Ouro Prêto, MG – 1814) – Architect and sculptor. The greatest personality in Brazilian art. 21, 22, 73

ALENCAR, José de (1829, Fortaleza, Ceará – 1877) – Writer, author of the romance *O Guarany*. 23

ALIBERTI, Alberto (1935, São Paulo, SP) – Painter and sculptor. 107

ALMEIDA, Guilherme de (1890, Campinas, SP-1969) – Poet. 24

ALMEIDA, Licinio de 1924, Vila da Feira, Portugal) – Designer. 88, 128

ALMEIDA PRADO, José Antônio (1943, Santos, SP) – Composer. 149

ALTBERG, Alexander (1908, Vienna, Austria) – Architect and engineer. Came to Brazil in the mid '30s. Designs and constructs houses in the rational style. In 1933, organizes the Exhibition of Tropical Architecture, Rio. 46, 48

ALVES DIAS, Gina (1929, Timbauba, PE) – Primitive art paintress. 21

AMADO, Jorge (1912, Pirangi, BA) – Writer. His work is the most translated of all brazilian writers. 145

AMARAL, Antonio Henrique (1935, São Paulo, SP) – Engraver and painter. 110

AMARAL, Tarsila do (1896, Capivari, SP) – Paintress. Studied in Paris after first World War, with Lhote, Léger and Gleizes. Later, she followed the theory of 'Antropofagismo', executing a series of paintings which plastically defined this movement. 26, 31

ANCHIETA, Padre José de (1533 Tenerife – 1597). 28

ANDRADE, Oswald de (1893, São Paulo, SP – 1954) – Poet, writer and critic. Outstanding personality of the 'Semana de Arte Moderna' (Modern Art Week, São Paulo, 1922). 24, 26, 31, 33

ANDRADE CAVALCANTI, Yonaldo (1933, Recife, PE) – Painter. He specializes in drawings of folkloric themes. 113

ANDRADE LIMA, Zazá (1922, São Paulo, SP) – Artistic designer. 108

ANDRADE Morais, Mario de (1893, São Paulo, SP – 1944) – Writer and poet. Excerted a decisive influence on the cultural renovation of his time, emphasizing on nationalism throughout his enthusiastic action, his writings and teachings. 23, 24, 26, 28, 33, 149

ANDRÉS, Maria Helena (1922, Belo Horizonte, MG) – Paintress. 121

ANDUJAR, Claudia (1931, Neuchâtel, Switzerland) – Photographer. Came to Brazil in 1955. She applies herself to the photography of native tribes. Contributor of *Life* and *Look* magazines. 133

APOLLINAIRE, Guillaume. 23

ARAGAO, Lyrio Dias (1933, Iripá, SP) – Cartoonist. 116

ARNOULT. Michel (1922, Paris) – Architect. Came to Brazil in the Fifties. Designs furniture. 139, 141

ARTIGAS, João Villanova (1915, Curitiba, PA) – Architect. Designs houses and important public works. Professor at the Faculty of Architecture and Urbanism of São Paulo. 66

ASKANAZY, Miecio (1911, Lemberg, Poland) – Art critic and ballet producer. Came to Brazil in 1939. In 1940, in Rio, he organized an exhibition of works condemned by the Nazi regime. From 1950 on, director of 'Braziliana', a folkloric dance and music group. 113

AUTUORI, Luiz Carlos (1941, São Paulo, SP) – Photographer. 128

B

BACH, Johann-Sebastian. 148

BAENDERECK, Sepp (1920, Hodasg, Yugoslavia) – Painter and advertising agent. Came to Brazil in 1948. 107

BAERLEIN, Group (1964, Rio de Janeiro, GB) Work team of industrial designers composed by Ronaldo Baerlein (1934, Rio de Janeiro, GB), and associates Leonardo Cavalleiro, Carlos Provenzano, Roberto Rodrigues Leite and Fernando dos Santos Lima. They design and produce objects of daily use in small series. 138

BANDEIRA, Antonio (1922, Fortaleza, CE – 1968) – Painter. In 1945, first trip to Paris, when he founds, with Bryen and Wols, the 'Banbryol group' of short duration, finishing when the latter dies. His works are the most original of all brazilian abstractionists. 119

BANDEIRA, Ladjane (1927, Nazaré de Mata, PE) – Paintress and playwright. 127

BANDEIRA, Manuel (1886, Recife, PE – 1968) – Poet. In 1913, when he met Paul Eluard, during a stay in a swiss sanatorium, he wrote his first poems. Later, he changed his style from symbolism to his last form of 'concretism'. He joined all the movements of renovation in the country. 33, 36

BARAVELLI, Luís Paulo (1942, São Paulo, SP) – Painter and sculptor. 89

BARBOSO, Augusto (1923, Alessandria, Italy) – Painter. Came to Brazil in 1957. Studied in Torino with Felice Casorati. 97

BARCELLOS Guerra Chaves, Vera (1938, Pôrto Alegre, RS) – Engraver. 113

BARRETO, Luís Carlos (1929, Sobral, CE) – Editor and photographer. Worked for the magazine *O Cruzeiro*. Later, directed the films *Assalto ao Trem Pagador* and *Vidas Sêcas*. 147

BARRIENTOS, Rodrigo (1933, Medellin, Colombia) – Painter.

Came to Brazil in 1961. Studied painting in Bogotá. 89

BARROS, Geraldo de (1923, Xavantes, SP) – Painter, photographer and industrial designer. 87, 139

BARROSO, Ary (1903, Ubá, MG – 1963) – Composer of popular music. Author of the famous song *Brazil (Aquarela do Brasil)*. 149

BARSOTTI, Hércules (1914, São Paulo SP) – Painter and industrial designer. 103, 126, 134

BARTHOLO, Maria Duarte (1933, Rio de Janeiro, GB) – Engraver. 111

BASÍLIO, Dora (1930, Rio de Janeiro, GB) – Engraver. 121

BASTOS, Carlos (1925, Salvador, BA) – Painter. He specializes on painting themes of life in Bahia. 115

BASTOS, Dorothy (1933, São Paulo, SP) – Engraver. 121

BASTOS, Maria Carmen (1935, Recife, PE) – Artistic designer. 109

BAUMGART, Emílio (1889, Blumenau, SC – 1943) – Engineer. Innovator in the field of concrete in Brazil. Constructs the first skyscraper in Rio. Made the calculations for the building of the Ministry of Education and Culture, Rio. 48, 49

BERNARDES, Sérgio Wladimir (1919, Rio de Janeiro, GB) – Architect. Author of many buildings and public works. 65, 66

BETTIOL, Zoravia (1935, Pôrto Alegre, RS) – Engraver. 100

BILL, Max. 84, 102

BISILLIAT, Maureen (1931, London, England) – Photographer. Came to Brazil in 1952. Studied painting with Lhote in Paris. Worked as photographer in New York. Co-author, with Roberto Santos and Marcelo Tassara, of the film *Roteiro de Guimaraes Rosa*. 133

BLANC, Carlos (1911, Iugos, Rumania) – Sculptor and painter. Came to Brazil in 1924. Obtains special technical skill working as craftsman on ironwork. 78

BO, Lina (1914, Rome, Italy) –

Architect. Came to Brazil in 1946. Former co-director of *Domus* magazine, Milan. In 1950, creates furniture. In 1964, founds the Museu de Arte Moderna da Bahia and restores the old 'Solar do Unhão' in order to open the Museu de Arte Popular, Salvador, Bahia. Designs and constructs, in 1959-1969, the new building of São Paulo's Museu de Arte. 13, 14, 62, 63, 84, 87, 137, 139, 143

BOCCHERINI, Luís. 149

BOCCHINO, Alceu Arioso (1918, Curitiba PA) – Composer. 149

BOESE, Henrique (1897, Berlin, Germany) – Painter. Came to Brazil in 1936, Studied with Kaethe Kollwitz. 98

BOLONHA, Francisco (1922, Belém, PA) – Architect. 67

BONADEI, Aldo (1906, São Paulo, SP) – Painter. 40

BONAZZOLA, Tiziana (1921, Varese, Italy) – Paintress. Came to Brazil in 1947. 96

BONDI Jardim, Freda (1936, Fortaleza, CE) – Mosaicist. Studies mosaic at the Academy of Ravenna. Returns to Brazil and founds a school for mosaics in Rio. 136

BONOMI, Maria (1935, Meina, Italy) – Engraver, costume and stage designer. 121

BOPP, Raul (1898, Santa Maria, RS) – Poet and diplomat. 24

BORSOI, Acacio Gil (1925, Rio de Janeiro, GB) – Architect. 64

BOURDELLE, Antoine. 29

BRAGA, Lênio (1931, Ribeirão Claro, PR) – Painter and photographer. 133

BRAGA, Theodoro (1872, Belém, PA – 1953) – Painter. In his interesting decorations he employed native motives. 28

BRAHMS, Johannes. 149

BRANCUSI, Constantine. 23, 26

BRANDAO, Álvaro Apocalypse (1937, Ouro Fino, MG) – Graphic designer and painter. Studies with Guignard in Belo Horizonte. 109

BRANDAO, José Vieira (1911, Cambuquira, MG) – Composer. Expert on musical education. 149

BRANDAO CELA, Raimundo (1890, Camocim, CE – 1954) – Painter and engraver. Worked lonely in his native town, painting historical and festive scenes. 22, 28

BRANNINGAN, Sheila (1914, Chester, England) – Paintress. Came to Brazil in 1957. Began to paint in Switzerland and later in Paris. In Brazil, from figurativism she turns to abstractionism. 120

BRAZIL, Alvaro Vital
see VITAL BRAZIL

BRATKE, Osvaldo (1907, Botucatu, SP) – Architect. 59

BRECHERET, Victor (1894, São Paulo, SP – 1955) – Sculptor. Studied sculpture with Arturo Dazzi in Rome, later in Paris. In São Paulo, for public gardens he executes several sculptures with stylish figures of decorative form and two monuments, 'Os Bandeirantes' and 'Duque de Caxias'. 30, 36, 45, 73

BRECHT, Bertold. 143

BRENNAND, Francisco (1927, Recife, PE) – Ceramist and Painter. 137

BRILL Czapski, Alice (192, Cologne, Germany) – Paintress and photographer. Came to Brazil in 1934. Studied with Erich Brill, her father. Used to photograph and paint while travelling throughout the country. 96

BRITO, Saturnino Nunes de (1914, Rio de Janeiro, GB) – Architect. 37, 49, 71

BRITO E CUNHA, João Carlos (1884, Rio de Janeiro, GB – 1950) – Illustrator. Elegant caricaturist of great popularity. 29

BUENO de Aguiar, Ely (1923, Rio de Janeiro, GB) – Engraver. 108

BUFFONI, Bramante (1912, Giulianova, Italy) – Painter and graphic designer. Came to Brazil in 1953. A famous graphic artist from Milan. At present, works for Olivetti in São Paulo. 129

BURLE MARX, Roberto (1909, São Paulo, SP) – Painter and landscape architect. Studied painting in Rio, later dedicated himself to botanical studies and garden architecture. Designed several importants gardens and parks in the country and abroad. 37, 44, 72, 137

C

CABOT, Roland (1929, Rio de Janeiro, GB) – Sculptor. In 1953, studied architecture in Paris, and engraving in New York, in 1962. Returned to Brazil in 1966. 83

CABRAL DE MELO NETO, João (1920, Recife, PE) – Poet, writer and diplomat. 143

CABRAL, Pedro Alvares (1467, Belmonde, Portugal – 1520) – Navigator, discoverer of Brazil. 22

CAESAR, Julius. 26

CALASANS NETO, José Julio (1932, Salvador, BA) – Engraver. 111

CALDEIRA FILHO, João da Cunha (1900, Piracicaba, SP) – Musical critic. Columnist of O Estado de Sao Paulo newspaper. 37

CAMARA Filho, João (1944, João Pessoa, PB) – Painter. 110

CAMARGO, Iberê (1914, Resinga Sêca, RS) – Painter. After studying architecture in Pôrto Alegre in 1947, he went to Rome to study painting with De Chirico and later on with Lhote in Paris. 119

CAMARGO, Sérgio (1930, Rio de Janeiro, GB) – Sculptor. Studied with Pettoruti and Lucio Fontana. In 1948, went to Paris and met Brancusi, Arp and Vantongerloo. In 1950, returned to Brazil. 1951 to 1953 worked and lived in Europe. Back to Rio, opened a studio and an art gallery with his brother. In 1961, moved to Paris, where he still lives. In 1963, received the award for sculpture in Paris IIIième Biennale. 81, 82

CAMARGO GUARNIERI, Mozart (1907, Tietê, SP) – Composer and conductor. 37

CAMPADELLO, Roberto (1942, Predazzo, Italy) – Painter. Came to Brazil in 1961. 94

CAMPOFIORITO, Quirino (1902, Belém, PR) – Painter, teacher and art critic. Columnist of Rio's newspaper O Jornal. 38

CAMPOS, Dileny (1942, Belo Horizonte, MG) – Painter and sculptor. Specialized in plastic-made objects. 83

CAMPOS MELLO, Sérgio de (1932, Rio de Janeiro, GB) – Painter. Lives in Paris. 121

CAMUS, Albert. 143

CAPANEMA, Gustavo (1900, Pitangui, MG) – Writer and politician. Former Minister of Education and Culture. 29, 36

CARAM, Marina (1925, São Paulo, SP) – Paintress and engraver. 89

CARDOSO AIRES, Lula (1910, Recife, PE) – Painter. Travels to Europe. Returns to Rio where he works for magazines and the theatre. In 1933, he is back in Recife, studying very closely the regional folklore which he exploits for his paintings and murals. 33, 113

CARDOSO AYRES, Emílio (1890, Recife, PE – 1916) – Cartoonist. Studied in Rio, Recife and Paris. Traveled alternately to Europe and Tunisia. Works as social caricaturist. Cooperated with Paris Le Rire and Gazette du Bon Ton. 24, 85

CARDOSO, Joaquim (1897, Recife, PE) Engineer and poet. See NIEMEYER

CARELLI, Antonio (1926, Mombuca, SP) – Mosaicist and painter. 136

CARIBÉ, pseudonym of Heitor Bernabó (1911, Lanus, Argentine) – Painter. Came to Brazil in 1939. In his work he reproduces the folklore of Bahia, which is his permanent theme. Executed a fresco for the American Airline Building at Idlewild Airport of New York, in 1959. 113, 136

CARLOS ESTÊVAO Souza (1921, Recife, PE) – Cartoonist. His popular work appears in Rio's magazine O Cruzeiro. 115

CARNEIRO, Dulce (1929, Atibaia, SP) – Photographer. 128

CARTEL, Louis-Bertrand. 104

CARVALHO, Flávio Rezende de (1899, Amparo da Barra Mansa, RJ) – Architect and painter. In England, studied architecture, at the same time dedicating himself to expressionistic painting and to highly skilled drawings. Due to his polemics of sociological character, Le Corbusier called him a 'revolutionary romantic'. 26, 27, 32, 48, 73

CARVALHO Muricy, Dinorah de (1905, Uberaba, MG) – Composer and teacher. 37

CARVALHO, Ronald de (1893, Rio de Janeiro, GB – 1935) – Poet. Began as parnassian poet; later wrote poems full of panamerican inspiration. 24

CASATI, G.M., architect. 55

CASSIANO RICARDO, Leite (1895, São José dos Campos, SP – Poet. 24

CASSOU, Jean. 6

CASTRO, Wagner de (1917, Franca, SP) – Painter. In an analitical and concise form, he paints symbolic subjects. He is one of the rare representatives of symbolism in Brazil. 108

CASTRO, Willys de (1926, Uberlândia, MG) – Painter and industrial designer. 103, 126

CASTRO ALVES, Antonio (1847, Cachoeira, BA – 1871) – Poet. Author of lyrical and epical poetry. Took important part in the social movement against slavery. 23

CAUDURO, João Carlos (1935, Sao Paulo, SP) – Architect and industrial designer. 141

CAVALCANTI, Alberto (1897, Rio de Janeiro, GB) – Film director. Graduated in architecture in Geneva. Worked initially as interior decorator. In Paris, from 1922 on, he is dedicated to cinematography; first as assistant to L'Herbier and later as independent film director and producer in France and England. In 1948, came to Brazil to direct the Vera-Cruz Motion Picture Company in São Paulo. After it was closed he returned to Europe, where he lives. 145, 146

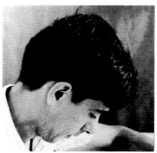

CAVALCANTI, Newton (1930, Bom Conselho, PE) – Engraver. Pupil of Goeldi. 111

CAVALLEIRO, Leonardo, see BAERLEIN.

CAYMMI, Dorival (1914, Salvador, BA) – Composer and singer of popular music. 149

CELSO Antonio de Menezes (1897, Caxias, MA) – Sculptor. Studied in Paris with Bourdelle. Born of native parents, he specialized in sculpture of indian figures when he returned to Brazil. His 1944's 'Mother' gave him a certain fame in the country, but today only a few connoisseurs still remember him. 29, 43

CELSO, Barbosa (1944, Rio de Janeiro, GB) – Cartoonist. 108

CENDRARS, Blaise. 26

CÉZANNE, Paul. 51

CHABAS, Paul. 33

CHAROUX, Lothar (1912, Vienna, Austria) – Painter. Came to Brazil in 1928. 107

CHARTUNI, Maria Helena (1942, São Paulo, SP) – Paintress. 6, 95

CHATEAUBRIAND Bandeira de Mello Assis (1891), Umbuzeiro, PB – 1968) – Journalist. Founder of Diarios Associados, newspaper, radio and television chain, in Brazil. Founder of the Museu de Arte, São Paulo. 51

CHAVES, Paulo (1927, Iguape, SP) – Engraver. 121

CHEVAL, Monsieur. 44

CHIAVERINI Ferrari, Miriam (1940), São Paulo, SP) – Engraver. 89

CHUST, Alberto (1934, Barcelona, Spain) – Photographer and graphic designer. Came to Brazil in 1947. 128, 129

CID de Souza Pinto, Bernardo (1925, São Paulo, SP) – Painter. Gave up his career as electronics engineer to dedicate himself to painting, developing a very communicative surrealistic graphism. 99

CLARK, Lygia (1920, Belo Horizonte, MG) – Sculptress. Began as a painter and later became a sculptress. Founded in 1959 with other artists the Neoconcreto group in Rio. Constructs objects of multi changeable shapes and forms. 105

COMBES, Abbé (born in France) – Photographer. Worked during the first half of the XIX century in this field. In 1839, arrived in Rio on board the 'L'Oriental', a ship best described as a floating university. First person to take up photography in Brazil. 84

CORDEIRO, Waldemar (1925, Rome, Italy) – Painter. Came to Brazil in 1947. Former follower of Concretism; later Pop-artist, mixing both tendencies in a way which he calls 'Pop-creto'. 88

CORINTH, Lovis. 26

CORRÊA DE ARAUJO, Pedro (1930, Recife, PE) – Goldsmith. Studied ceramics in Denmark, but upon his return to Brazil he set to work in jewelry. 137

CORREA LIMA, Atílio (1901, Rome, Italy – 1943) – Architect and urbanist. Came to Brazil in 1924. Expert in city planning, in 1940 designed and constructed Rio's Port for Hydroplanes. Ahead of his times, he reached a structural and traditional solution by applying the 'helicoidal scale', which later on would become one of the characteristics of brazilian architecture. 37, 57

CORTEZ, Jaime (1926, Lisbon, Portugal) – Designer. Came to Brazil in 1947. Author of the book Técnica do Desenho, 1965. 116, 126

COSME, Luís (1908, Pôrto Alegre, RS) – Composer. 149

COSTA, Claudio Manoel da (1729, Mariana, MG – 1789) – Poet and patriot. Committed suicide in prison. 22

COSTA, Lúcio (1902, Tolone, France) – Architect and urbanist. After his first studies in

England and Switzerland he graduated in architecture in Rio. From 1920 on, with José Mariano, he leads a movement for the study and interpretation of forms and ideas of colonial architecture. In 1930, he is invited to reorganize the S.B.A. (Brazilian Society of Architecture). He is regarded as the outstanding leader of the renewal of brazilian architecture, assimilating and adopting the technical innovations with great sensibility and personal touch in favor of formal purity. He designed the pilot plan for Brasilia. 35, 36, 44, 45, 46, 48, 50, 52, 54

COSTA, Waldemar da (1904, Belém, PR) – Painter and teacher. Studies painting in Lisbon and Paris. Teaches painting in Brazil, forming several good and successful artists. His work gradually changes from figurative to abstract-geometric. 102

COUTINHO, HEITOR (1926, Belo Horizonte, MG) – Sculptor. Works in plastic-made objects. 83

CRAVO, Mario (1923, Itajipa, BA) – Sculptor. Good craftsman in varied sculpture techniques. Studied with Mestrovic in New York. From a primitive expressionist fase he changes his work, eventually following, in his particular way, the latest art trend abroad. 78

CRISTOFANI, Telesforo (1929, Viareggio, Italy) – Architect. Came to Brazil very young. 71

CROCE, Benedetto. 22

CRUZ, Carmélio (1924, Canindé, CE) – Painter. 96

CRUZ, Roberto (1931, Belém, PR) – Architect. 71

CUNHA, Euclydes da (1866, Cantagalo, RJ – 1908) – Writer. Military engineer, author of *Os Sertoes (The Backlands)*, war diary of Canudos, masterwork of Brazilian literature. 28

D

DA COSTA, Maria Leontina (1917, São Paulo, SP) – Paintress. Studies painting in São Paulo. After a period of figurative painting, searching the substance of form, her rich imagination leads her to the lyrical interpretation of a geometrical world. 102

DACOSTA, Milton Rodrigues da Costa (1915, Niterói, RJ) – Painter. Abandons law studies to dedicate himself to painting. In a later fase, his works acquired a strong symbolic form of metaphysical and post-cubistic impressions. 102

D'AMICO Fourpone, Teresa (1919, São Paulo, SP – 1965) – Paintress. In Paris, studies sculpture with Zadkine and Zorach. During a sojourn abroad she abandons sculpture for painting and collage, using elements of popular art and Brazilian foklore 21

DEBUSSY, Claude. 23

DE CASTRO, Amilcar (1920, Belo Horizonte, MG) – Sculptor and graphic designer. Studied and worked in Rio. Lives in New York. 105

DE CHIRICO, Giorgio. 26

DE FIORI, Ernesto (1884, Rome, Italy – 1945) – Sculptor and painter. Came to Brazil in 1936. After having won fame in Berlin as one of the most active and lively sculptors at that time he came to live and work in São Paulo. There he devoted his activity mainly as portraitist and also as figure and landscape painter, but never reached the fame enjoyed before. 43

DEL PICCHIA, Menotti (1893, São Paulo, SP) – Writer, poet and painter. One of the leaders of 'Semana de Arte Moderna' (Modern Art Week). Author of *Juca Mulato*, a popular book. 24

DELAMONICA, Roberto (1933, Ponta Porã, MT) – Engraver. Studied with Friedländer. In 1957 he starts travelling, visiting the Orient, Europe and South-American countries. At present lives in New York, where he works and teaches. He is considered a paragon of a conscientious artist, always improving his techniques. 117

DENIS, André (1906, Calais, France) – Architect and sculptor. In Paris, studied architecture; sculpture with Maillol. Came to Brazil in 1945. 74

DI CAVALCANTI, Emiliano (1897, Rio de Janeiro, GB) – Painter. He abandons his law studies to draw caricatures and illustrate books. After World War I, in Paris he becomes acquainted with Fauvism and Cubism, which he combines with much originality, depicting the popular life of Brazil. He is also the author of many decorative paintings, panels, mosaics and tapestry. 24, 26, 33, 36, 124

DIAS, Antonio (1944, Campina Grande, PB) – Painter. Artist who unconsciously paints in the style of Pop art, but still maintains alive sharp impressions of his childhood spent at his home town. Lives in Paris. 91

DIAS, Cicero (1907, Jundiá, PE) – Painter. Studies architecture in Rio. As a painter, he first followed his candid impulses, painting scenes from the life of his native states, full of imagination and pathetic poetry. Moved to Paris in 1938, where

he lives. There, after a surrealistic experiment and followed by a geometrical abstract painting, he reached a rather informal style. At present he works in an urbane figurativism mode. 32, 39, 85

DJANIRA, da Motta e Silva (1914, Avaré, SP) – Paintress. Using painting as a pastime, she is noted for her natural and personal style of rare originality, outstanding in the numerous group of primitive painters. Later she adopted a heraldic style in which forms and colours are simplified. 19

DOMINGO, Francisco (1893, Barcelona, Spain) – Painter. Came to Brazil in 1950. In 1913, moved to Paris where he struck a friendship with Picasso, Miro and Gris, becoming their faithful follower. In 1932, returned to Barcelona. 98

DOMINICI, Enrico (1909, Bologna, Italy) – Industrial designer. Came to Brazil in 1946. Specializes in designing and producing lighting fixtures. 138

DOUCHEZ, Jacques (1921, Maçon, France) – Painter and tapestrymaker. Came to Brazil in 1950. Lived and studied in Paris. First dedicated to painting and later, associated with Nicola, to weaving artistical and original tapestries. 137

DUARTE, Anselmo (1920, Itú, SP) – Actor and film director. In 1962, plays the leading role and directs *O Pagador de Promessa*, the film that won the Golden Laurel at the Cannes Festival in the same year. 145, 147

DUBUGRAS, Victor (1868, La Flexe, France – 1933) – Architect and teacher. Came to Buenos Aires and there graduated in architecture. In 1891, came to São Paulo, where he teached and worked as an architect in Art Nouveau style. 34

DUCHAMP, Marcel. 82

DUPRAT, Régis (1930, Rio de Janeiro, GB) – Composer. 149

DUPRAT, Rogério (1932, Rio de Janeiro, GB) – Composer. 149

DYER, Charles. 130

E

EBLING, Sônia (1926, Pôrto Alegre, RS) – Sculptress. Studied in Pôrto Alegre, later on with Zadkine in Paris. Starting from a figurative basis she slowly accomplished an informal style. 78

EICHBAUER, Hélio (1941, Rio de Janeiro, GB) – Stage designer. Studied painting in New York and scenography in Prague. 144

EISENSTEIN, Sergej. 145

ESMERALDO, Servulo (1929, Crato, CE) – Engraver. Studies with Friendländer, in Paris, where he lives. 113, 127

F

FAJARDO, Carlos Alberto (1941, São Paulo, SP) – Painter and sculptor. 95

FEIJÓ, Hélio (1913, Recife, PE) – Painter and Architect. Inventor of an air-conditioning system. 38, 48

FERNANDEZ, Millôr (1923, Rio de Janeiro, GB) – Cartoonist, play-wright and humorist. His draw-ings are of great originality and his humoristic compositions are endorsed with a sense of hu-manity. Critic of human fail-ures and candor. Writes daily chronicles with a great sense of humour. Author of *Tempo e Contratempo* and lately, in coo-peration with Rangel, of *Liber-dade, Liberdade* a play. 115, 129

FERRARI, Donato (1933, Guar-diagrele, Italy) – Painter and sculptor. Came to Brazil in 1960. He uses assorted materials in his abstract-expressionistic works. 82, 83, 127

FERRAZ, Geraldo (1906, Campos Novos de Paranapanema, SP) – Journalist and art critic. Colum-nist of the newspaper *O Estado de Sao Paulo*. 27

FERREIRA FILHO, Jeferson (1930, Cassia dos Coqueiros, BA) – Cartoonist. 130

FERREIRA GULLAR, pseudonym of Ribamar Ferreira (1930, São Luiz, MA) – Poet, writer and art critic. In 1959, co-founder and theorist of neoconcrete art movement, Rio. 80, 105

FERRO Simone Pereira, Sérgio (1938, Curitiba, PR) – Painter, architect. Teaches History of Art at the Faculty of Architec-ture and Urbanism of São Paulo. 71, 92

FIAMINGHI, Hermelindo (1920, São Paulo, SP) – Painter and advertising agent. 107

FICKER-Hoffman, Lisa (1879, Leipzig, Germany – 1962) – Paintress. Came to Brazil in 1914. Studied in her home town. From 1930 to 1933, worked in Paris, then returned definitively to Brazil. 38

FIGUEIRA, Joaquim Lopes (1907, São Paulo, SP – 1943) – Sculptor and painter. 42

FIGUEIREDO FERRAZ, José Carlos de (1918, Campinas, SP) – Engineer. Inventor of a process for pre-stressed concrete, first applied in the construction of São Paulo's Museu de Arte building. 63

FLEXOR, Samson (1907, Sareka, Rumania) – Painter. Came to Brazil in 1947. Studied painting in Paris and Brussels. In São Paulo where he still lives, work-ed as portraitist and fresco painter in academic style. Later he changed to geometric ab-stract and afterwards to informal decorative painting. At present works on figurativism. 98

FORTUNA, Reginaldo José (1931, São Luis, MA) – Caricaturist. 115

FRANÇA, José Augusto (1925, Tomar, Portugal) – Art critic. A scholar very interested in brazilian art. Visits Brazil often. Co-operator of *Colóquio*, Lisbon, and *Art d'Aujourd'hui*, Paris. 19

FREITAS, Agostinho Batista de (1927, Campinas, SP) – Painter. An electrician who started paint-ing spontaneously, chosing as theme the streets and squares of São Paulo, also sights and scenes of the outskirts of the town. 21

FREITAS, Ivan (1930, Rio de Janeiro, GB) – Painter. 101

FREUD, Sigmund. 124

FREYRE, Gilberto (1900, Aflitos, Recife, PE) – Sociologist and writer. Scholar of international fame. Author of *Casa Grande e Senzala (Masters and Slaves)* and several works on Brazilian sociology. 30, 31, 32

FRISCH, Max. 143

FUKUSHIMA, Tikashi (1920, Fu-kushima, Japan) – Painter. Came to Brazil in 1940. 122

G

GALLET, Luciano (1893, Rio de Janeiro – 1931) – Composer. 149

GEELMUYDEN, Frederika (born in Norway) – Fashion creator. Worked in Brazil from 1967 to 1968. 134

GEIGER, Anna Bela (1933, Rio de Janeiro, GB) – Engraver. 113

GERCHMAN, Rubens (1942, Rio de Janeiro, GB) – Painter. Dedicated mainly to construc-tion of objects in a satyrical vein. 91

GIL Vicente. 143

GIMENEZ, M. Cinematographer. 147

GIORGI, Bruno (1903, Mococa, SP) – Sculptor. Studied in Paris at the Academie de La Grande-Chaumière. First, he worked in the heavy and volu-minous style of Maillol. Later he adopted the surrealistic way and finally changed to a threadlike form in which his Brasilia's monuments are executed. At present, he works in an impressi-ve non-objective language. 42

GISMONDI, Maria Cecília Ma-nuel (1928, Rio de Janeiro, GB) – Paintress. 96

GLEIZES, Albert. 27

GNATTALI, Radamés (1906, Pôrto Alegre, RS) – Composer and conductor. 149

GOBBIS, Vittorio (1894, Treviso, Italy – 1968) Painter. 37

GOELDI, Oswaldo (1895, Rio de Janeiro, GB – 1961) – Engraver. Son of the Swiss scientist Emil Goeldi, founder of the famous Botanical Museum of the Ama-zon River, 'Museu Goeldi', in Belém. He studied in Switzer-land and came under the influen-ce of Kubin (1877-1959), whose art also influenced Paul Klee. Returning to Brazil after World War I, his strict european educa-tion suffered the impact of tropical climate, finding its manner in his sharp expressionis-tical woodcuts which depict popular scenes of Rio and its environs. 39

GOLYSCHEF, Jef (1897, Kherson, USSR) – Painter. Came to Brazil in 1957. After studying music and painting in Odessa he emigrated to Germany where he figured in 1914 among the first dodecaphonists. There he joined the German dadaist movement with Hausmann and Huelsen-beck. In 1933, the Nazi regime destroyed his work. In Brazil, he returned to his interrupted activity. 98

GOMES, Carlos (1836, Campinas, SP – 1896) – Composer. Follow-ing the school of Verdi, he wrote the opera *O Guarani*. 149

GOMEZ DA CRUZ, Joseph. 19

GOMIDE, Antonio Gonçalves (1895, Itapetininga, SP – 1967) – Painter. In 1913, moved to Geneva, Switzerland. From 1914 to 1918, studied with Gillard and Hodler. In 1920, moved to Paris, where he met Lhote, Picasso, Braque, Picabia, Seve-rini and the film director Alber-to Cavalcanti. In that period, his work is strongly done in the cubist principle but in a personal way. In 1929, after a brief visit to Europe, he finally settled down in Brazil, where he was very active as an artist and sometimes as a teacher, leaving an impor-tant work. 34

GONÇALVES DIAS, Antonio (1823, Caxias, MA – 1870) – Poet and playwright. One of the greatest Brazilian poets, he evoked and idealized in his works the aborigines' life and customs. 23

GONÇALVES DE MAGALHÃES, Do-mingos José (1811, Rio de Janei-ro, GB – 1882) – Diplomat, poet and writer. With Gonçalves Dias and Apolinario Pôrto Ale-gre made the romantic trium-virate of brazilian Romantism. 28

GONZAGA, Tomás Antonio (1744, Pôrto, Portugal – 1810) – Poet and patriot. 22

GOODWIN, Philip L. 44, 47

GOROVITZ, Mona (1937, Cruz Alta, RS) – Paintress. Designs fashion and sometimes composes objects of pop-art tendency. 88, 135

GRAÇA ARANHA, José Pereira de (1868, São Luiz, MA – 1930) – Poet and dramatist. A romantic writer notwithstanding his aver-sion to romanticism. Participates in 'Semana de Arte Moderna' (Modern Art Week), in 1922. 24, 28

GRACIANO, Clovis (1907, Araras, SP) – Painter. Follows in a later period the manner and themes of Portinari, but in a very personal way. He is considered the greatest mural painter in Brazil. 40

GRASSMANN, Marcello (1925, São Simão, SP) – Engraver. Dedicat-ed himself spontaneously to engraving and drawing, choos-ing creatures of phantasy as his favourite subjects. His supreme skill wins him the well-deserved fame as the greatest designer and engraver of the country. 109

GRAZ, John (1891, Geneva, Switzerland) – Painter, decora-tor and architect. Came to Brazil in 1922, joining the 'Semana de Arte Moderna'. 37

GRINOVER, Lucio (1934, Trieste, Italy) – Architect and in designer. Came to Brazil 1950. 130, 138

GRIS, Juan. 27

GROHMANN, Will. 26

GROPIUS, Walter. 84

GROVELLI, Graziella. 10

GRUBER Correia, Mario (1927, Santos, SP) – Painter and en-graver. Studied engraving with Poty. In 1950, went to Paris, studying painting with Goerg. Later on, with Portinari and Di Cavalcanti. He is dedicated to painting fantastic folkore-related themes. 115

GUEDES, Joaquim (1932, São Paulo, SP) – Architect. 68

GUELLER, Sylvia Mara (1942, São Paulo, SP) – Engraver. 107

GUERRA PEIXE, Cesar (1914, Petrópolis, RJ) – Composer and conductor. 149

GUERRA, Noêmia (1920, Rio de Janeiro, GB) – Paintress. Studied with Lhote in Paris, where she lives since 1958. Her work displays a tendency towards abstractionism. 120

GUERRA PEIXE, Cesar (1914, Pe-trópolis, RJ) – Composer and conductor. 149

GUEVARA, Andres (1899, Villeta, Paraguay – 1964) – Graphic ar-tist. Came to Brazil in 1923. Worked as layoutman on several newspapers and magazines and proved to be a subtle and sarcas-tic caricaturist. 36

GUIGNARD, Alberto da Veiga (1895, Nova Friburgo, RJ – 1962) – Painter. Studied painting in Munich and Florence, and returned to Brazil about 1930. Moved to Belo Horizonte MG, where he opened an art School attended by most of the nu-merous artists of the region. 39

GUIMARAES, João (?) – Painter. 33

GUIMARAES ROSA, João (1909, Cordisburgo, MG – 1968) – Writer and diplomat. A con-spicuous storyteller, of powerful strength, writing in a unique style. Author of *Grande Sertao: Veredas (Devil to pay in the Backlands)*, *Sagarana*, etc. 13, 33

GUIOMAR NOVAES, Pinto (1895, São Paulo, SP) – Pianist. 37

GUTIERREZ, Antonio Carlos (1935, Itaqui, RS) – Painter. 115

H

HAENDEL, George-Frederick. 149
HANSEN-'Bahia', Karl (1915, Hamburg, Germany) – Engraver. Came to Brazil in 1948. Influenced the painters of Bahia, especially by his engraving technique. In 1958, returns to Germany and later goes to Ethiopia, to teach at the Addis Abeba's Art School. 111
HARNISCH, Sacha (1920, Florence, Italy) – Photographer. Came to Brazil in 1946. Lives in Rio. 133

HENRIQUE, Gastão Manuel (1933, Amparo, SP) – Painter. Lately, he is dedicated to the construction of solid geometrical objects. 82, 83
HERING, Elke (1940, Blumenau, SC) – Sculptress. Studies in her home town; from 1958 to 1960, in Munich with Anton Hiller. 76
HIRSCH, Eugenio (1923, Vienna, Austria) – Painter and photographer. Came to Brazil in 1965. Studied under Kokoschka. Lived for some time in Argentine. Cooperated with international magazines with his photographs and drawings of much imagination. Heads the art department of *El Mundo de los Museos* collection, published by Codex, Buenos Aires, with some co-editions in Europe. At present, he lives in Madrid. 109
HORA, Abelardo da (1924, São Lourenço, PE) – Sculptor. 74

I–J

IANNI, Octávio (1926, Itú, SP) – Essayist and professor of sociology. Teaches at the University of São Paulo. 57
IMPÉRIO, Flávio (1935, São Paulo, SP) – Stage and costume designer. Architect and occasional painter. 92, 143
ITIBERÊ, Brasílio (1896, Curitiba, PR) – Composer. 149
ITO, Tadayoshi (1919, Mie, Japan) – Sculptor. Came to Brazil in 1959. Studied sculpture in Japan. In São Paulo, opened a ceramic workshop. 122
JAGUAR, pseudonym of Sérgio Jaguaribe (1932, Rio de Janeiro, GB) – Cartoonist. Abandons his law studies and starts drawing. Co-operates with *Senhor* and *Manchete* magazines. 115, 126, 127, 130
JAMMES, Francis. 24
JANNELLI, Arcangelo (1922, São Paulo, SP) – Painter. Studies with W. da Costa. After working exclusively in figurativism, changes to abstractionism. 113
JARDIM, Evandro Carlos (1935, São Paulo, SP) – Engraver. 99
JARDIM, Luís (1901, Garanhuns, PE) – Illustrator. 33
JASMIN, Luís (1940, Salvador, BA) – Painter and actor. 134
JAVUREK, Miroslaw (1916, Letovice, Czechoslovakia) – Photographer. Came to Brazil in 1952. As cinematographist, specialized in short-length films. 9
JOBIM, Antonio Carlos 'Tom' (1927, Rio de Janeiro, GB) – Composer of popular music. 149

K

KAFKA, Franz. 126
KATO, Ariaki (1931, São Paulo, SP) – Architect. 60
KAZMER, Fejer (1922, Pecs, Hungary) – Sculptor. Came to Brazil in 1949. 107
KEATING, Luís Antonio Vallandro (1940, Rio de Janeiro, GB) – Painter. 100
KEFFEL, Eduardo (1903, Speyer, Germany) – Photographer. Came to Brazil in 1936. Since his youth dedicated himself to the cinema and to newspaper reporting. In Brazil, he organizes the photographic services of *O Cruzeiro* magazine. 62
KIDDER SMITH, G.E. 44
KING, Betty (1932, New Orleans, U.S.A.) – Paintress. Came to Brazil in 1955. 96
KLIASS, Rosa Grena (1932, São Paulo, SP) – Landscape designer and architect. 57
KONDER, Leandro. 80

KONDO, Bin (1937, Anton, Mandchuria) – Painter. Came to Brazil in 1960. Studied painting in Tokyo. 122

KRAJCBERG, Frans (1921, Kozienice, Poland) – Painter. Came to Brazil in 1949. In 1945, abandons his studies of engineering in Leningrad, moving to Stuttgart; becomes pupil of Willy Baumeister. In Brazil, he lived in the Parana's hinterland. In 1958, moved to Paris, where he still lives. 79, 82
KRIEGER, Edino (1928, Brusque, SC) – Composer. 149
KÜHN, Heinz (1908, Berlin, Germany) – Painter. Came to Brazil in 1950. 107

L

LACERDA, Osvaldo (1927, São Paulo, SP) – Composer. 149
LADEIRA, Iracy de Assis (1919, Uberlândia, MG) – Primitive painter. 19
LANZELLOTI, José (1926, São Paulo, SP) – Cartoonist. 116
LÁU, Percy (1906, Arequipa, Peru) – Painter. Came to Brazil very young. Specializes in painting the brazilian rural life. 38
LAZZARINI, Domenico (1920, Camaiore, Italy) – Painter. Came to Brazil in 1951. 120
LAZZAROTTO, Poty (1924, Curitiba, PA) – Engraver and teacher. Distinguishes himself in the techniques of graphic arts. From 1950 to 1953, directs the engraving studio of the Museu de Arte of São Paulo. 111
LE CORBUSIER. 29, 37, 44, 47, 49, 50
LEAO, Carlos Azevedo (1906, Rio de Janeiro, GB) – Architect and painter. Took part in the team that designed and built the Ministry of Education and Culture in Rio. 36, 50
LEAO, Maria Luisa (1932, Rio de Janeiro, GB) – Paintress. Pupil of Portinari. 96
LEE, Wesley Duke (1931, São Paulo, SP) – Painter and graphic designer. First worked in graphic arts, later on in painting as representative of 'Magic realism'. At present, designs decorations and constructs objects. 78, 89, 127, 141
LEFÈVRE, Rodrigo Brotero (1938, São Paulo, SP) – Architect. 71
LEGER, Fernand. 26, 27, 36
LEIRNER, Felicia (1904, Warsaw, Poland) – Sculptress. Came to Brazil in 1927. Studied sculpture with Brecheret in São Paulo. From a work almost entirely devoted to the human figure she changed to free forms. 73
LEIRNER, Nelson (1932, São Paulo, SP) – Painter. Applies himself with dedication to the most extreme and controversial experiences. 93
LEITE, Roberto Rodriguez, see BAERLEIN.

LEMOS, Fernando (1926, Pôrto, Portugal) – Painter and graphic designer. Came to Brazil in 1950. 104, 135
LEOPARDI, Giacomo. 78
LÉRY, Jean de (1534, La Margelle, France – 1613) – Calvinist preacher. Author of a travel book *Histoire d'une voyage fait en terre du Brésil*, 1577. 85
LEVI, Livio Edmondo (1933, Trieste) – Architect, industrial designer and goldsmith. Came to Brazil in 1939. Teaches industrial design at the faculty of architecture and urbanism of São Paulo. Lately, he is emerging as an interesting jewel designer. 137
LEVI, Rino (1901, São Paulo, SP – 1965) – Architect. Graduated in architecture in Rome. In Brazil, became known through many of his projects, designed in the spirit of his times, creating a seriousness in his uncompromised work. In 1942, elaborated the São Paulo's 'Sedes Sapientiae' Institute of Philosophy. Later he specialized in designing bank buildings and hospitals. 34, 46, 66
LEWY, Walter (1905, Oldesloe, Germany) – Painter. Came to Brazil in 1937. He paints in a distinct surrealistic way. Owns a large collection of Cactus plants. 108
LIMA BARRETO, Victor (1906, Casabranca, SP) – Film director and producer. Author of *O Cangaceiro*, in 1953. 145
LINS DO RÊGO, José (1901, Pilar, PB – 1957) – Writer. 145
LISBÔA, Antônio Francisco, see ALEIJADINHO.
LIPCHITZ, Jacques. 45
LIZARRAGA, Antonio Gundemaro (1920, Spain) – Industrial designer and illustrator. 138
LONGHI, Roberto. 97
LONGO, Eduardo (1942, São Paulo, SP) – Architect. 68

M

MABE, Manabu (1924, Kumamoto, Japan) – Painter. Came to Brazil in 1934. Came to the country to work in a farm. Autodidact. Arriving in São Paulo he attains fame very quickly as figurativist and later as abstractionist, winning many national prizes. 78, 122, 123

MACHADO, Jorge Moreira (1904, Paris, France) – Architect. Came to Brazil very young. 36, 50, 69
MACIEL, Valdeir Oliveira (1937, Bacabal, MA) – Painter. 104
MAGALHAES, Fabio (1942, São Paulo, SP) – Painter. 94
MAGALHAES, Roberto (1940, Rio de Janeiro, GB) – Engraver and painter. 111
MAGNELLI, Aldo (1902, Florence, Italy) – Engineer. 141
MAIA, Antonio (1928, Carmópolis, SE) – Painter. Autodidact. Works in the mystic tradition of religious popular art. 21
MALFATTI, Anita (1896, São Paulo, SP – 1964) – Paintress. First studies with her father and later in Berlin with Lovis Corinth. Returns to Brazil as an expressionist. In 1917, in São Paulo, she opens her first exhibition considered to be very 'revolutionary' due to the polemical character of the works exhibited. Later on, after the conspicuous initial fase, she reached an ordinary folklorism that ever since marked all her production. 26, 32
MALLARMÉ, Stephane. 23
MANGE, Ernesto Roberto de Carvalho (1922, São Paulo, SP) – Engineer and urbanist. 60
MANOEL VICTOR, Filho (1927, São Paulo, SP) – Cartoonist. 126
MANTEGNA, Andrea. 51
MANZON, Jean (1916, Paris, France) – Photo-reporter. Came to Brazil in 1944. During World War II works for *Paris Match*. Since 1950, producer of short-length films. Chief-photographer of *O Cruzeiro* magazine. 10, 84
MARCIER, Emeric (1916, Cluj, Rumania) – Painter. Came to Brazil in 1940. Studies in Milan. Dedicated to mural painting, he has done the decoration of the 'Capela da Juventude Trabalhadora' in Mauá, SP. 115
MARINETTI, F.T. 24
MARIO DE ANDRADE, see ANDRADE Morais, Mario de.
MARIZ, Vasco (1921, Rio de Janeiro, GB) – Diplomat and musician. Scholar of history of music. Author of a bio-bibliographical dictionary of music.

148, 149
MARQUES de Souza, Sérgio (1918, Rio de Janeiro, GB) – Engineer. 59
MARTIM GONÇALVES, Eros (1920, Recife, PE) – Scenographer and stage director. 14, 130, 143
MARTINS, Aldemir (1922, Juguazeiras, CE) – Painter. 113, 135
MARTINS, Luís (1907, Rio de Janeiro, GB) – Writer. Columnist of *O Estado de Sao Paulo*. 27
MARTINS, Maria (1900, Campanha, MG) – Sculptress. 42, 73
MARTINS, Rubens de Freitas (1929, São Paulo – 1968) – Industrial designer. Begins to paint in 1959, later he applies himself solely to industrial design. 126, 128, 138
MATISSE, Henri. 51
GREGORIO DE MATTOS (1633, Salvador, BA – 1696) – Poet. The first social-minded poet of a lyrical and satyrical vein. 22
MAUAD MEALE, Group (1967, Rio de Janeiro, GB) – Work team of architects and furniture designers composed of Jorge Jabour Mauad (1933, Providência, MG) and Osiris Cunha Meale (1935, Cachoeiro do Itapemirim, ES) 139
MAURÍCIO DE NASSAU, João (1604, Dillenburg, Germany – 1679) – Governor of Brazil's Northeast during the Dutch conquest and Captain-general and Admiral of the West Indies Company. 84
MAURO, Humberto (1898, Volta Grande, MG) – Film director. Pioneer of brazilian cinematography. In 1925, he made *Valadao* and *A Cratera*, in 1937, *Discovery of Brazil*, with music by Villa-Lobos; of remarkable importance and notable influence in the country. 145, 146
MAVIGNIER, Almir da Silva (1925, Rio de Janeiro, GB) – Painter, graphic designer and teacher. Studied painting in Rio; in 1952 goes to Paris. Pupil of Max Bill in Ulm's 'Hochschuhle für Gestaltung', specializing in graphic design. Lives and teaches in Hamburg. 104
M'BOY, pseudonym of Cássio (1903, Mineiros do Tietê, SP) – Primitive painter. 21
MEDEIROS, José (1923, Teresina, PI) – Photographer and film director. Director of short-length films, endowed with an acute sense of observation. 133
MEIRELLES, Heli Lopes (1917, Ribeirão Prêto, SP) – Lawyer and teacher. 57
MEIRELLES, Victor (1832, Florianópolis, SC – 1903) – Painter. Worked for Pedro II court; painted scenes of historical events and places. 149
MELLO FRANCO de Andrade, Rodrigo de (1898, Belo Horizonte, MG - 1969) – Historiograph. Founder and director of S.P.H.A.N., Service for Protection of Historical and Artistical Patrimony. 33
MELLO, Manuel Messias de (1935, Maceió) – Designer. 16
MENDES, Sérgio (1941, Niterói, RJ) – Musical group director and composer of popular music. Lives in New York. 149
MENTZ, Suzana (1939, Pôrto

Alegre, RS) – Paintress. 121
MERQUIOR, J.G. (1941, Rio de Janeiro, GB) – Writer and diplomat. 24, 80
MESTRINER, Odila (1928, Ribeirão Prêto, SP) – Paintress. 96
METRO 3 (1964, São Paulo, SP – 1968) – Work team of industrial and graphic designers composed of Petit and Zaragoza. 131
MICHAINOVICH, Armando (1938, Buenos Aires) – Designer. 128
MIGNONE, Francisco (1897, São Paulo, SP) – Composer. 37, 149

MILLER, Luiza (1922, Rio de Janeiro, GB) – Sculptress. Studied with Zadkine in Paris, where she lives. 78
MILHAUD, Darius. 149
MILLIET da Costa e Silva, Sergio 1898, São Paulo – 1967) – Writer, poet and painter. Highly cultured and active person and forerunner of the modernistic movement in art. 27, 37
MINDLIN, Henrique Ephim (1911, São Paulo, SP) – Architect. Expert in history of architecture in Brazil. 71
MIRANDA, Alcides da Rocha (1909, Rio de Janeiro, GB) – Architect and painter. Dedicated to the teaching and restoration of antique architecture. 46
MOHALYI, Yolanda Lederer (1909, Kolozsvar Cluj, Hungary) – Paintress. Came to Brazil in 1931. 113
MOJICA, Marin José (1929, São Paulo) – Producer and director of films. 147
MONDRIAN, Piet. 27
MONTE, Maurício (1928, Fortaleza, CE) – Architect. Designs and produces furniture in small series. 138
MONTEIRO, Vicente do Rego (1899, Recife, PE) – Painter and poet. Lived in Recife and Paris, alternately. Around 1920, participated in the post-cubist movement and created in his works engine-like forms of much vigour. In 1924, illustrated *Legendes et Croyances-talismans des Indiens de l'Amazonie*, Paris. He is much appreciated in the field of French poetry. In 1960, won the 'Prix Apollinaire'. Lives and teaches in Brasilia. 30, 33
MONTEIRO DA SILVA CRUZ, Vera Ilce (1942, São Paulo, SP) – Architect and Paintress. 94
MONTEIRO LOBATO, José Bento (1882, Taubaté, SP – 1948) – Writer and sociologist. 26
MORAES, Avatar (1933, Bagé, RS) – Painter. Dedicated to the construction of objects. 82
MORAES, Bernardo Ribeiro – Lawyer. 57

MORAIS, P.V. de. 127
MORAIS, Vilma Martins (1934, Belo Horizonte, MG) – Engraver and costume designer. 121
MORAIS, Vinicius de (1913, Rio de Janeiro, GB) – Poet, diplomat and composer of popular music. 149
MORI, Jorge (1932, São Paulo, SP) – Painter. Excellent copyist of masterwork paintings of the Renaissance. 96
MORPURGO, Vittorio. 46
MOTTA LIMA, Ubirajara (1930, São Paulo, SP) – Architect and painter. 89
MOURAO, Caio (1933, São Paulo, SP) – Goldsmith. Studied painting with Bonadei in 1956. 137
MOURAO, Noêmia (1918, São Paulo, SP) – Paintress and illustrator. Pupil of Di Cavalcanti. 32
MUSSOLINI, Benito. 22, 46

N

NADAR, nickname of Feliz Tournachom. 24
NAPOLEON. 26
NASSER, Frederico Jayme (1945, São Paulo, SP) – Painter. 92
NASSIF, Wilson Georges (1946, Rio de Janeiro, GB) – Engraver and illustrator. 111
NAZAR, Teresa Nazar (1936, Mendoza, Argentine) – Paintress. Came to Brazil in 1960. 92
NEPOMUCENO, Alberto (1864, Fortaleza, CE – 1920) – Composer. 149
NERI, Wega (1916, Corumbá, MT) Paintress. 113
NERY, Ismael (1900, Belem, PA – 1934) – Painter. Studied with little enthusiasm at the 'Escola de Belas Artes', Rio. Leaves for Paris, where he becomes acquainted with Picasso and Chagall. Shows interest in poetry and all branches of plastic arts, including industrial design, interior decoration and fashion. His strong personality influenced Di Cavalcanti, Portinari and Rio's artistic circles of his time. 29, 34
NICOLA, Noberto (1931, São Paulo) – Tapestry maker. 137

NIEMEYER Soares Filho, Oscar (1907, Rio de Janeiro, GB) – Architect. The most popular architect of Brazil whose most outstanding work is the Government buildings of Brasília, the new capital. The engineer Joaquim Cardoso solves to utmost perfection the structure problems. 35, 36, 41, 44, 50, 52, 81

NOBILING, Elisabeth (1902, São Vicente, SP) – Engraver, designer and ceramist. 136
NOBRE, Carlos (1939, Recife, PE) – Composer. 149
NOGUEIRA LIMA, Maurício (1930, Recife, PE) – Architect and painter. 89
NUNES GARCIA, Padre José Maurício (1767, Rio de Janeiro, GB – 1830) – Composer. Jesuit priest, inspector of music at the 'Capela Real do Rio de Janeiro', known for his *Missa de Santa Cecilia*. 148

O

ODRIOZOLA, Fernando (1921, Oviedo, Spain) – Painter. Came to Brazil in 1953. 101

OHTAKE, Ruy (1938, São Paulo, SP) – Architect. 71

OHTAKE, Tomie (1913, Kyoti, Japan) – Paintress. Came to Brazil in 1936. Begins to paint in 1952. Lately, in her works she uses large areas of pure color. 122, 123

OITICICA, Hélio (1939, Rio de Janeiro, GB) – Sculptor. Began as a concretist painter. At present, joins the 'Tropicalia', group in searching for new artistical experiments. 105

OLIVEIRA, Raimundo de (1930, Feira de Santana, BA – 1966) – Painter. Artist of popular formation. He worked exclusively on biblical themes in a genuine mystical style, which reminds of medieval stained glass. 21

OLIVEIRA, Sara Ávila de (1932, Nova Lima, MG) – Engraver. 121

OSTROWER, Fayga (1920, Lodz, Poland) – Engraver and teacher. 113

OSWALD, Carlos (1882, Florence, Italy) – Engraver and teacher. Came to Brazil in 1910. Introducer of the art of modern engraving in the country. He forms two generations of engravers. 38

OSWALD, Henrique (1854, Rio de Janeiro, GB – 1931) – Composer. 149

OTAVIO Câmara de Oliveira (1930, Rio de Janeiro, GB) – Humorist and newspaper illustrator. Very popular through his vignettes and stories on sport. 115

OVALLE, Jaime (1894, Belém, PA) – Composer. 149

P

PAES LEME, Bella (1920, São Paulo, SP) – Stage and costume designer. First studied painting in Paris, later changed to scenography. 143

PALATNIK, Abram (1928, Natal, RN)-Painter. Studies first in Tel-Aviv and upon returning to Brazil in 1948 starts constructing light projecting machines in continuous movement, and works in industrial design. In 1962, he produces a patented new technique of spacial perception called 'Perfect square' 104.

PALMA, Maria (1906, Vacaria, RS) – Paintress. Autodidact working on popular themes. 19

PANCETTI, José Giannini (1902, Campinas, SP – 1958) – Painter. Joined the Navy, and later dedicated himself to seascape painting, producing works of a picturesque sensibility. 39

PARREIRAS, Antônio (1860, Niterói, RJ – 1939) – Painter. His home town dedicates a museum to his art. 25

PARRELLA, Lew (1927, New Haven, Conn., USA) – Photographer. Came to Brazil in 1961. Director of photography, Editora Abril, São Paulo. Picture editor and exhibitions planner. 127

PASQUALINI, Wilma (1930, Rio de Janeiro, GB) – Paintress. Studies with Friedländer, in Rio. 89

PEDRO AMERICO de Figueiredo e Mello (1843, Areias, PB – 1905) – Painter. Studied painting in Paris with Ingres. Interested in literature, natural science and politics. Author of many paintings celebrating the Independence of Brazil. 23, 149

PEDROSA, José Alves (1915, Rio Acima, MG) – Sculptor. 80

PEDROSO D'HORTA, Arnaldo (1914, São Paulo, SP) – Painter and journalist. 100

PEIXOTO, Alvarenga (1744, Rio de Janeiro – 1793) – Patriot. 22

PEIXOTO, Mario (1905, Rio de Janeiro, GB) – Cinematographer, produced Limite, an important motionpicture. However, he never more worked in cinematography. 145, 146

PENNA, Alceu (1916, Curvelo, MG) – Fashion and costume designer. 134, 135

PENNACHI, Fulvio (1905, Lucca, Italy) – Painter. Came to Brazil in 1929. Studied in Florence. In Brazil, worked in fresco paintings for churches. In his works he brings out aspects of everyday life in

subtle tones. 40

PENTEADO, Darcy (1926, São Roque, SP) – Painter, stage and costume designer. 115

PENTEADO, Olívia Guedes (1872, Campinas, SP – 1934) – Patroness of the arts. Lived in São Paulo. In the first decades of the century, traveling frequently to Europe, she brought to Brazil an important collection of avant-garde art works. 26, 36

PEREIRA DOS SANTOS, Nelson (1928, São Paulo, SP) – Journalist and film director. Directed the film Vidas Sêcas. 13, 147

PERET, Benjamin. 107

PERETTI, Marianne (1927, Paris, France) – Paintress. Came to Brazil in 1953. 113

PEREZ, Rossini Quintas (1932, Macaiba, RN) – Engraver. Studied with Ostrower and Friedländer. From 1953 on is dedicated to engraving. Lives in Paris. 117

PÉRICLES Maranhão de Andrade (1924, Recife, PE – 1961) – Caricaturist. During almost 20 years, he has drawn one of the most popular comic figures 'O Amigo de Onça' (The Tiger's Friend) for O Cruzeiro magazine. 115

PERISSINOTO, Alexandre José (1925, Mococa, SP) – Graphic designer. 128

PERSIO, Lôio (1927, Tapiratiba, SP) – Painter. 113

PERSON, Luís Sérgio (1936, São Paulo, SP) – Cinematographer. Film director of 'São Paulo S.A.'. 147

PETIT Reig, Franciso (1934, Barcelona, Spain) – Graphic design. Came to Brazil in 1952. 141

PICASSO, Pablo. 23, 26, 27, 51

PIGNATARI, Décio (1927, Jundiaí, SP) – Poet and essayist. Dedicated to the problems of communication. 128

PILÓ, Conceição (1929, Belo Horizonte, MG) – Engraver. 120

PINTO ALVES, Carlos (1888, São Paulo, SP – 1967) – Writer. Animator of the arts in São Paulo. 37

PINTO Alves, Mussia (1900, Sebastopol, Russia) – Sculptress and goldsmith. 37

PIZA, Arthur Luiz (1928, São Paulo, SP) – Engraver. Studies in his home town. In 1951, he moves to Paris, where he improves his engraving techniques with Friedländer. In order to obtain new plastic values, he starts engraving in an 'à gaufrage' process. Alongside this new engravings he created the fascinating mosaics of colourful cardboard pieces. 119

PIZZI, Orlando (1931, Santos, SP) – Cartoonist. 116

POETZCHER, Maria Victoria (1938, Rio de Janeiro, GB) – Artistic designer. 108

POIRET, Paul. 23

POLETTI, Ruggero (1929, São Paulo, SP) – Painter. Works in Milan but visits Brazil frequently. He acquires a profound knowledge of Italian art of the last four centuries, mainly from the regions of Lombardy and Venice. In his paintings he manifests the purest figurativism, accentuating his thematical se-

lection with a rare sense of everyday events. 97

POLLOCK, Jackson. 78

POLO, Maria (1937, Venice, Italy) – Paintress. Came to Brazil in 1959. 113

PONS, Isabel (1912, Barcelona, Spain) – Engraver. Came to Brazil in 1948. Studies painting in her native town. In Brazil she illustrates many of Garcia Lorca's works and designs costumes for Marcel Camus' Black Orpheus. 101

PONTUAL, Arthur Lício (1935, Recife, PE) – Architect and industrial designer. 139

PORTINARI, Cândido (1903, Brodósqui, SP – 1962) – Painter. Pupil of 'Escola de Belas Artes' in Rio, and later one of its teachers. In 1928, visited Europe, where he learned the technique of fresco painting which later he applied in his important historical and allegorical cycles at Rio's Ministry of Education and Culture, the Washington Library of Congress, and later on, in oil on canvas, in the mural of the UNO building in New York. He was an indefatigable painter of Brazilian popular life. 29, 30, 41, 44, 124

POST, Franz (1612, Leyden, – Holland – Painter. Worked for the Prince Maurice of Nassau's court in Brazil. 84

PRADO, Carlos (1908, São Paulo, SP) – Architect and painter. Participated in the new trend which arose after the 'Semana de Arte Moderna'. 39

PRADO, Paulo (1869, São Paulo, SP – 1943) – Farmer and businessman. Author of the essay Retrato do Brasil (Portrait of Brazil). Promoted the immigration of European labour based on social, sociological and historical principles. 24

PRADO, Vasco (1914, Uruguaiana, RS) – Sculptor. In Paris, studied painting with Léger and later engraving. When he returned to Brazil changed to sculpture. 74

PRAZERES, Heitor dos (1898, Rio de Janeiro, GB – 1967) – Painter and composer of popular music. From 1937 on he began painting popular themes and those of the Rio's slums. Very typical in his portrayal of the popular customs, animator of folklore and cultivator of afro-brazilian

traditions, he composed songs and founded in Rio an 'Escola de Samba' (a sort of a samba association) movement. 19, 149
PROVENZANO, Carlo, see BAERLEIN.
PUTZOLU, Efisio (1930, Rome, Italy) – Sculptor. Came to Brazil in 1960. From radio and TV repairman starts out as Pop-art sculptor. 82

Q-R

QUADROS, Anna Letícia (1929, Teresópolis, RJ) – Engraver. 121
QUEIROZ, Eça de. 140
RAMOS, Graciliano (1892, Quebrangulo, AL – 1953) – Writer. Author of *Memorias do Cárcere* and *Vidas Sêcas*, describing the life and problems of the people of his native region. 147
RAMOS DE AZEVEDO, Francisco (1851, São Paulo, SP – 1928) – Construction engineer. Graduated in Brussels. Returned to Brazil where he designed and constructed in an eclectical style. 27, 34
RAMOSA, Edival (1940, Rio de Janeiro, GB) – Painter. Lives in Italy since 1964 and adheres to Pop-Art. 107
RAUSCHENBERG, Robert. 78
RAVEL, Maurice. 23
REA, James (1940, Jubblepore, India) – Painter and graphic designer. Came to Brazil in 1964. 92
REBÔLO Gonzales, Francisco (1903, São Paulo, SP) – Painter. Very active artist in the 'Família Artística Paulista'. 40
REIDY, Afonso Eduardo (1909, Paris, France – 1964) – Architect. Came very young to Brazil. A disciple of Le Corbusier; ardent defender of modern architecture. As officer of Rio's Municipality he planned and designed the popular housing project of Pedregulhos, which is his best work. Belonged to the work team which designed and constructed the Ministry of Education and Culture, Rio. Among his outstanding achievements Rio's 'Museu de Arte Moderna' buildings. 36, 50, 66
RESENDE Filho, José de Moura (1945, São Paulo, SP) – Painter and sculptor. 93
REY, Ruben (1931, São Paulo, SP) – Painter. 82
RIBEIRO COUTO, Rui (1898, Santos, SP – 1963) – Poet. 24
RIBEIRO, Jesuino (1935, Guaxupé, MG) – Painter. Studied with Goeldi in Rio. His drawings are full of a definite trend towards sarcasm in the social realm. 101
RISSONE, Paolo (1925, Reggio Calabria, Italy) – Painter. Came to Brazil in 1948. In his work he represents natural elements in an abstract form. 110
RIVERA, Diego. 29
ROBERTO, Irmãos (1942, Rio de Janeiro, GB) – Architecture team work. Composed of the brothers Marcelo, Mílton and Maurício, known as the MMM group, considered one of the most serious and original in the country. 37, 49, 66
ROBERTO, Marcelo (1908, Rio de Janeiro, GB – 1964) – Architect. 37, 49, 66
ROBERTO, Maurício (1921, Rio de Janeiro, GB) – Architect. At present, director of the Rio's 'Museu de Arte Moderna'. 37, 49, 66
ROBERTO, Mílton (1914, Petropolis, RJ – 1953) – Architect. 37, 49

ROBERTO CARLOS Braga (1941, Cachoeiro do Itapemirim, ES) – Singer and composer of popular music. 93, 148, 149
ROCHA, Glauber (1939, Vitória da Conquista, BA) – Film director and playwright. Author of *Deus e o Diabo na Terra do Sol* (1964) and other films. One of the 'nouvelle vague' precursors in the national cinematography. Author of the book *Revisao critica do Cinema Brasileiro*, 1963. 13, 146, 147
RODIN, Auguste. 23
RODRIGUES, Glauco (1929, Bagé, RS) – Painter. Worked in graphic arts on the staff of editors of *Senhor* magazine. 104, 120
RODRIGUES, Hugo (1929, Buenos Aires, Argentine) – Sculptor. Came to Brazil in 1962. Began as a painter and later turned to sculpture. In Rio, follows the trend of 'Art brut'. 76

RODRIGUES, Sérgio (1927, Rio de Janeiro, GB) – Architect. Specialized in furniture design. 139
ROSA, Noel (1911, Rio de Janeiro, GB – 1937) – Composer of popular music. 149
ROSSELLINI, Roberto. 145
ROSSI, Alícia (1928, Buenos Aires, Argentine) – Paintress. Came to Brazil in 1963. 107, 137
ROSSI, Guglielmo. 13
ROSSI OSIR, Paulo (1890, São Paulo, SP – 1959) – Painter. Studied painting in Milan and Paris. Returned to Brazil where he revived the use and application of decorated glazed tiles. 40
ROUSSEAU, Jean-Jacques. 104
RUCHTI, Irene (1931, Laguna, SC) – Landscape designer. 72
RUCHTI, Jacob (1917, Zurich, Switzerland) – Architect. Came to Brazil in 1919. 71
RUDGE, Antonieta (1886, São Paulo) – Pianist and teacher. 37
RUDOFSKY, Bernard (1907, Zanchtel, Austria) – Architect. Came to Brazil in 1938. Graduated as architect in Rome. In 1941 he went to New York, where he still lives and works. A scholar of art literature and author of the book *Are clothes modern?* 46, 47

S

SALGUEIRO, Maurício (1930, Vitória, ES) – Sculptor. Studies in Rio. Undertakes very advanced experiments in 'art brut' applying it very often to sound elements. 80

SAMICO, Gilvan José Meira Lins (1928, Recife, PE) – Engraver. Studied with Goeldi. His woodcuts are of an archaic and popular type, marked by a serious composition, an acute imagination and a clean technique. 8, 113
SANOVICZ, Abrahão (1933, Santos, SP) – Architect and industrial designer. 57, 126
SANTA ROSA Junior, Tomas (1909, João Pessoa, PB – 1956) – Painter and stage designer. Since his boyhood painted banners for religious celebrations. Arrived in Rio in 1932, becoming one of Portinari's faithful followers. One of the most dynamic elements of the Rio's artistic life. 110
SANTIAGO, Manoel de Assumpção (1897, Manáus, AM) – Painter. Studies in Rio. His post-impressionistic work is linked to the remembrance of stories and legends of the Amazon region. 28
SANTORO, Cláudio (1919, Manáus, AM) – Composer. 149

SANTOS, Agnaldo dos (1926, Gamboa de Itapecirica, BA – 1962) – Sculptor. Carved figures of an expressionistic character, with much simplicity, accentuating a primitivism of African origin. His spontaneity and his very personal expression produced the most original sculptures of his region. 74
SANTOS, Roberto (1928, São Paulo, SP) – Cinematographer. 147
SANTOS LIMA, Fernando dos, see BAERLEIN.
SAPIA, Batistesa (1924, Paysandu, Uruguay) – Painter. Came to Brazil in 1965. 109

SAPIA, Hector (1930, Buenos Aires, Argentine) – Painter. Lives in Brazil and Italy. 94
SARACENI, Paulo César (1933, Rio de Janeiro, GB) – Cinematographer. Wrote the script of the film *Porto das Caixas*. 147
SASSON, Daniel (1921, Paris, France) – Enamelist; see Sasson, Renée.
SASSON, Renée (1922, Ellisville, USA) – Enamelist. Came to Brazil in 1953. Married to Daniel. After studies in Paris and Limoges, the couple came to Brazil. They design and produce many kinds of enameled objects in a perfect technique, of highly esthetic quality. 136, 137
SAYDEBERG, Luis Simoes (1939, Piracicaba, SP – Graphic designer. 116
SCHAEFFER, Frank (1917, Belo Horizonte, MG) – Painter. Studies in Paris under Léger and Lhote. Travels through Europe and South America. He reaches a refinement in his artistical expression. 120
SCHEIER, Peter (1908, Glogau, Germany) – Photographer. Came to Brazil in 1937. Author of various photographic albums on Brazil. 53

SCHENDEL, Mira (1919, Zurich, Switzerland) – Paintress. Came to Brazil in 1949. 89
SHIMITZU, Takeo (1935, Dairen, Mandchuria) – Sculptor. Came to Brazil in 1961. Studied sculpture in Japan. 76
SCHULTZ, Harald (1909, Pôrto Alegre, RS – 1966) – Ethnologist. Scholar of great value, author of *Hombu*, a book on brazilian indians.
SCLIAR, Carlos (1920, Santa Maria, RS) – Painter. 115
SEELINGER, Helios Aristides (1878, Rio de Janeiro, GB – 1965) – Painter. As a caricaturist works for popular magazines in Rio. 29
SEGALL, Lasar (1891, Vilna, USSR – 1957) – Painter. Studied with Liebermann in Berlin. In 1913, visited Brazil for the first time, organizing exhibitions of his works in São Paulo and Campinas. After World War I, in Germany, he distinguished himself as one of the most active and original expressionists. Attracted by the tropics and its people, he returned to São Paulo, where he lived and worked. The Museum Lasar Segall in São Paulo is dedicated by his family to his works and memory. 26, 35, 36, 37, 73, 84
SERPA, Ivan Ferreira (1923, Rio de Janeiro, GB) – Painter. Studies with Leskoschek. After

a short interlude of 'constructivism', the prehistoric cave paintings, seen during a trip to Europe, exercise great influence on him. He returns to figurative painting and through personal research reaches a world of fantasy. 94

SHIRO TANAKA, Flavio (1928, Sapporo – Hokaido, Japan) – Painter. Came to Brazil in 1933. Self-taught. In 1953, after working in São Paulo, he goes to Paris where he studies mosaics with Gino Severini and engraving with Friedländer. At present lives in Paris, where he carries out his work as a painter. 122

SILVA, Benjamin (1927, Juazeiro, CE) – Painter. 92

SILVA, Emanuel Bernardo da (1939, Moreno, PE) – Sculptor. 21

SILVA, Francisco Domingos da (1910, Alto Tejo, AC) – Painter. 21

SILVA, José Antonio da (1909, Salles de Oliveira, SP) – Painter. The most popular of the primitive art painters. 7, 19, 51

SILVA, Quirino da (1902, Rio de Janeiro, GB) – Painter and art critic. 27, 32

SILVA, Sérgio Vicente da (1938, Franca, SP) – Advertising agent. Works as art director. 126

SILVEIRA, Regina Scalizilli (1939, Pôrto Alegre, RS) – Paintress. 100

SILVEIRA MELLO, Ennes (1932, São Paulo, SP) – Architect. 71

SIQUEIRA, José Batista (1907, Conceição, PB) – Composer and conductor. 149

SMYTHE, Eska (1909, Warsaw, Poland) – Sculptress and paintress. Came to Brazil in 1939. Studied in Warsaw and Vienna. She made several statues for public squares, portraits and large bas-reliefs in Brazil. At present lives in Paris. 120

SOUZA, Gerson de (1926, Recife, PE) – Primitive painter. 20

SOUZA, Jarbas José de (1937, Uberaba, MG) – Painter. 128

SOUZA, José Maria de (1935, Valença, BA) – Painter. Draws pathetic and romantic characters. 100

SOUZA, Mauricio (1935, Santa Izabel, SP) – Cartoonist. 116

SOUZA, Waldomiro de Deus (1944, Boa Nova, BA) – Primitive art painter. 21

SOUZA LIMA João de (1908, São Paulo) – Composer and conductor. 37

SOUZA SOARES, Manoel Alberon de (1934, Massapé, CE) – Graphic designer. Works in the printing shop of the University of Ceará. 113

STOCKINGER, Francisco (1919, Traum, Austria) – Sculptor. Came to Brazil very young. Studies sculpture with Giorgi. In 1954 he moves to Pôrto Alegre, where he teaches and makes statues of a very strong expression of human grief. 77

STUPAKOFF, Otto (1935, São Paulo, SP) – Photographer. Studies photography at Los Angeles' Art Center School. In 1966, went to work in New York, where he still lives. 133

SUZUKI, João (1935, Mirandopolis, SP) – Painter. 122

SZPIGEL, Samuel (1936, Rio de Janeiro, GB) – Architect and painter. 92

T

TANAKA, Beatriz (1932, Salvador, BA) – Costume designer. Lives in Paris. 143

TAVARES, Heckel (1928, Natal, RN) – Composer. 149

TEIXEIRA, Alberto Dias (1925, São João do Estoril, Portugal) – Painter. Came to Brazil in 1950. Studied painting in Lisbon. 107

TENIUS, Carlos Gustavo (1939, Pôrto Alegre, RS) – Sculptor. Studied sculpture in his native town. 80

TERUZ, Orlando (1902, Rio de Janeiro, GB) – Painter. His work is based on the expression of popular themes. 39

TESTORI, Giovanni. 97

THIOLLIER, René (1884, São Paulo, SP – 1968) – Essayist. Author of the book A Semana de Arta Moderna. 24

THOMAS, Ayrton (1934, Rio de Janeiro, GB) – Cartoonist. 116

TIAGO, Sebastião Ferreira de Amorim (1943, Limoeiro, PE) – Painter and ceramist. 96

TIRADENTES, nickname of Joaquim José da Silva (1746, Sitio Pombal, MG – 1792) – Martyr of brazilian independence. 30

TOMASO, Regina Carneiro (1929, Uberlândia, MG) – Fashion designer. 134

TOMOSHIGE, Kusuno (1935, Yubari-Hokkaido, Japan) – Painter. Came to Brazil in 1961. 88

TORRES, Caciporé (1932, Araçatuba, SP) – Sculptor. 75

TOSCANO, João Walter (1933, São Paulo, SP) – Architect. 71, 136

TOSCANO SETTI, Odiléa Helena (1934, São Bernardo do Campo, SP) – Architect. She is dedicated to graphic arts. 127

TOYOTA, Yutaka (1931, Yamagata, Japan) – Painter. Came to Brazil in 1960. Studied in Tokyo, where he became scenographer of the traditional Kabuki theatre. In Brazil, works as abstract painter. 122

TRIGUEIRINHO NETO (1931, São Paulo) – Cinematographer. 147

TRINDADE LEAL, Geraldo (1927, Santana do Livramento, RS) – Engraver. Prints album of his woodcuttings in a singular style. 108

U–V

UCHÔA, Helio (1925, Rio de Janeiro) – Architect. 37

ULMAN, Chinita. 37

VACCARINI, Bassano (1914, San Colombano al Lambro, Italy) – Sculptor and scenographer. Came to Brazil in 1946. Is established in Ribeirão Prêto. 88

VALENÇA LINS, Darel (1924, Palmeiras, PE) – Painter and engraver. 101

VALENTIM, Rubem (1922, Salvador, BA) – Painter. His works are inspired by afro-brazilian symbols. 107

VAN ACKER, José Antonio (1931, São Paulo, SP) – Painter. 89

VAN GOGH, Vincent. 51

VARGAS, Getulio (1893, São Borja, RS – 1954) – Former President of Brazil. 36, 44

VASCONCELLOS, Ernani (1912, Rio de Janeiro, GB) – Architect and painter. One of the team who designed Rio's Ministry of Education and Culture. 36, 50

VATER, Regina (1939, Rio de Janeiro) – Painter. 94

VELAZQUES, Glauco (1884, Naples Italy – 1913) – Composer. 149

VERGARA, Carlos Augusto (1941, Rio de Janeiro, GB) – Painter. 19

VERGER, Pierre 1902, Paris, France) – Sociologist. Came to Brazil in 1946. Author of many books on Latin America, among which Bahia de tous les poêtes.

VIANNA, Frutuoso (1896, Itajubá, MG) – Composer. 149

VICTOR, Manuel Filho (1927, São Paulo) – Designer. 116

VIGLIOLIA, Miguel Anselmo (1931, Buenos Aires, Argentine) – Industrial engineer and photographer. Came to Brazil in 1960. 133

VILLA-LOBOS, Heitor (1887, Rio de Janeiro, GB – 1959) – Composer and conductor. Transformed the authentical and creative values of brazilian folklore into an intense musical expression. 23, 33, 74, 145, 148, 149

VILELLA DE MORAIS, Paulo (1934, Rio de Janeiro, GB) – Architect and graphic designer. 127

VIRGULINO, Wellington (1929, Recife, PB) – Painter. 100

VISCONTI, Elyseu (1867, Salerno, Italy – 1944) – Painter. Came to Brazil very young. Studied in Rio and completed his formation in Paris, where he was attracted by Post-impressionism and by Art-nouveau. He excerted a sound influence as teacher on the later generation. 22, 28

VITAL BRAZIL, Álvaro (1909, São Paulo, SP) – Architect.

In 1937, with Adhemar Marinho, designs and constructs São Paulo's 'Esther' building, one of the most perfect constructions in the country. 37, 46

VITRAC, Roger, 143

VLAVIANOS, Nicolas (1929, Athens, Greece) – Sculptor. Came to Brazil in 1961. 75

VOLPI, Alfredo (1896, Lucca, Italy) – Painter. Came to Brazil in 1898, As a child began to work with his father, a contractor, doing ornamental wall painting. Later, and with much success, he applies himself to landscape and figure painting, focusing characteristic types and scenes of rural villages. After a long series of paintings where he gradually rationalizes the landscape and the folkloric symbols, slowly through a sequence of formal reductions, he reaches a thrifty language, which finally leads him to concretism. 40

VUILLARD, Edouard. 27

W

X-Y-Z